Contents

Introduction

This book sets out to explain the fundamental importance of elections in modern democracies and to identify the range of arguments surrounding their effectiveness. It also seeks to explore the relationship between citizens and politicians at election time, in an attempt to discover the motives behind voters' electoral behaviour.

Chapter 1 asks how compatible elections are with the concept of democracy. It is based on a discussion of the relative merits of different forms of democracy and an investigation into how various electoral systems attempt to perform the basic functions of democracy.

The second chapter takes the analysis of electoral systems further, investigating the desirability of electoral reform in the UK. By analysing the effects of the various systems used in the UK since 1997 and the response of the major political parties to the issue, it also considers the likelihood of an alternative system to first-past-the-post being used to elect MPs in future general elections.

Chapters 3 and 4 focus on the way that people behave during elections. While electoral behaviour was relatively easy to predict in the two decades after the Second World War, significant social changes contributed to a radical new way of explaining why people voted the way they did. Chapter 3 examines the many theories of voting behaviour, while Chapter 4 focuses on the impact that election campaigns have on the direction of the popular vote.

The final chapter considers a relatively specialised form of single-issue election, known as a referendum. It outlines the circumstances in which referendums take place, and provides an assessment of their strengths and weaknesses as democratic devices.

The terms in the glossary on pp. 105–107 have been highlighted in purple throughout the book for easy reference.

Elections are the only occasion when most people actively engage in the political process. However, recent elections have suggested that the number of people participating in elections is falling at a dramatic rate. I hope that this book is able to demonstrate why elections remain an essential part of the democratic process and are a fascinating subject for study.

Neil Smith

How effectively do elections promote democracy?

Democracy

Type the word 'democracy' in the search engine Google and tens of millions of entries will come up. Do the same with 'elections' and you will get approximately the same number of entries. However, type in the two terms together and only a tenth of that will show up. What does this tell us about the compatibility of democracy and elections? In one sense, it could mean that, in the modern era, elections matter more to people than democracy and that modern society has developed a fixation with processes rather than outcomes. In another sense, it could simply suggest that the internet is a pretty useless tool for providing simple answers to complex questions.

What is democracy?

The difficulty in answering this question lies in the fact that any definition depends entirely on when it is written or the time to which it is referring. Nowadays, for example, we would commonly associate phrases such as 'popular participation', 'the public interest' or 'political equality' with democracy, and as such we regard it as essentially a good thing.

However, this has not always been the case. In ancient Athens, democracy was more often regarded as something to be avoided. A number of classical scholars wrote at length on the apparent flaws with democracy. Aristotle defined 'rule of the people' as government by the propertyless, uneducated masses, who used power to serve their own ends, that is, to overtax the wealthy.

> It is manifest that the best political community is formed by citizens of the middle class, and that those states are likely to be well administered in which the middle class is large, for the addition of the middle class turns the scale, and prevents either of the

extremes from being dominant. Great then is the good fortune of a state in which the citizens have a moderate and sufficient property; for where some possess much, and the others nothing, there may arise an extreme democracy, or a pure oligarchy; or a tyranny may grow out of either extreme.

Aristotle, 'The polis', from Politics

Consequently, he regarded this kind of extreme democracy as an enemy of freedom. Instead, he advocated a government by the middle classes that allowed for political participation by all citizens. Socrates and Plato argued that the masses' lack of education would lead them into poor decision making and subservience to persuasive and unscrupulous demagogues.

The influence of the Greek anti-democrats was such that the term 'democracy' did not make a political comeback until the American War of Independence, which ushered in not only a new era of democracy, but also an entirely new form of democracy. Indeed, the modern interpretation can be traced back to Abraham Lincoln's justification for fighting the American Civil War in the Gettysburg Address.

Learning point

The Gettysburg Address, November 1863

> Four score and seven years ago, our fathers brought forth upon this continent a new nation: conceived in liberty, and dedicated to the proposition that all men are created equal...It is rather for us to be here dedicated to the great task remaining before us...that this nation, under God, shall have a new birth of freedom...and that government of the people...by the people...for the people...shall not perish from the earth.

In what ways did Lincoln contribute to the modern definition of democracy?

London Illustrated News

Abraham Lincoln

To what extent is there agreement on the merits of democracy?

In spite of its widespread use, not every political theorist has agreed that democracy is necessarily a good thing. Up until the nineteenth century, the term was used pejoratively to describe a state of 'mob rule'. An outline of the main debate over the concept's strengths and weaknesses is provided in Table 1.1.

Table 1.1	Merits and criticisms of democracy

Merits	Criticisms
Social democrats It fosters a sense of community.	*Plato* Some people are not capable of governing themselves.
Locke It enables citizens to check power of government.	*De Tocqueville* Majority rule ignores the wishes of significant minorities.
Rousseau The ability to make one's own laws makes man truly free.	*Michels* True democracy is impossible to achieve as power always ends up in the hands of a wealthy, well-organised elite.

Task 1.1

(a) Explain what you understand by the term 'tyranny of the majority'.

(b) Describe three ways in which citizens in the UK can check government power.

Guidance

(a) This term describes one of the principal flaws with democracy. As it is based on the notion of majority rule, it rarely takes into account the interest of large minorities. This is particularly an issue where the majority is very small. A good example of this is when a plurality system is used to elect a president, as illustrated by the results of the 2004 US presidential election. Given the 'winner takes all' nature of the election, the size of the victory margin is irrelevant; the only important issue is who gets the most votes.

US presidential election, 2004	
George W. Bush	50.7%
John Kerry	48.3%

(b) First, citizens can vote governments out. The usual way for governments in the UK to fall is by losing a general election. This last occurred in 1997, when the Conservative administration was overwhelmingly voted out of office.

Second, citizens exercise control through parliament. The electorate votes for an MP, who has a range of scrutinising devices at his or her disposal. These include oral and written questions, and the select and standing committee system.

Third, citizens are able to use the courts to hold the government to account. The process of judicial review investigates whether government decisions were reached fairly.

What forms of democracy exist?

Democracy is a 'contested concept', in that there are a range of interpretations of what it actually stands for. The main argument is between supporters of **direct democracy** and those of **representative democracy**, and revolves around the extent of popular participation in the democratic process.

Direct democracy

In this model, citizens participate directly in the government of the state, thus creating genuine government 'by the people'. This idea of mass participation was epitomised by the Athenian model of democracy (see Box 1.1).

While direct democratic theories differ in the extent to which they prescribe legislative and executive power, the key point is that citizens can directly participate in the political decision-making process. Modern direct democracy can be found in several forms, as outlined below.

> **Box 1.1**
>
> **Athenian democracy**
>
> - Began around 508 BC.
> - 30,000 citizens in Athens.
> - Assembly met 40 times a year.
> - 5,000 citizens would attend each meeting.
> - Members of the ruling council of 500 selected by lot.

Referendums

The referendum is the most commonly used form of direct democracy, and few countries that claim to possess democratic credentials operate without at least occasional resort to one. Voters are asked to state whether they agree or disagree with a proposal, and the result can either bind or merely inform the actions of the government. The referendum is widely used in town or state-level politics in the USA, and has been increasingly used at regional and local level in the UK since 1997.

Initiatives

An initiative is a form of citizen-initiated referendum that aims to introduce a new law or overturn an existing one. South Dakota was the first US state to introduce the initiative, in 1898, and since then a few other states have followed suit. In Switzerland, the government is forbidden from holding plebiscites, and the only referendums held are at the behest of citizens. In this sense, the use of initiatives most closely resembles a pure model of direct democracy, since the government has no power to distort or abuse the referendum process for its own ends. The average Swiss citizen can expect to participate in six elections and 30 initiatives in a single year.

Given the UK's historical antipathy to referendums, it is not surprising that few initiatives have been held here. In 2003, the government actually removed the right of Welsh citizens to request a vote on the sale of alcohol on a Sunday. Previously, temperance movements could request a vote if they obtained the support of either 500 registered voters or a county borough.

Local consultative referendums

Several MPs have carried out surveys of popular opinion in order to gauge the mood of their constituents either on controversial issues such as ID cards, or on an issue likely to affect the local community, such as the construction of a new bypass or airport runway.

Recall elections

A recall election is the rare practice of using popular votes to hold individual politicians to account. Typically, advocates of the recall need to acquire the support of 20–25% of the people who originally voted for a public official to trigger the special election. Arguably the most famous example of this took place in California in October 2003 when Gray Davis became only the second governor in US history to be recalled from office. Voters rejected him after complaints of fiscal incompetence, and replaced him with Hollywood action hero Arnold Schwarzenegger. Even national leaders can be subject to the recall: in August 2004, Hugo Chavez, the president of Venezuela, survived a referendum after opponents had triggered a recall election earlier in the year.

Selection of juries

Not often regarded as an example of democracy in action, the selection of juries has much in common with the selection of the ruling councils in ancient Greece. Citizens are chosen at random by computer from electoral rolls to sit in judgement of their peers.

Electronic voting

In politics and business, **electronic voting (e-voting)** is frequently used to gauge public opinion. Quicker and less expensive than paper ballots, it has proved successful in providing an almost instant poll on a proposed law or business plan. Recent examples have included the internal consultative poll by the Manufacturing, Science and Finance (MSF) trade union to get feedback from employees on its intended merger with the Amalgamated Engineering and Electrical Union. It has even been suggested that its use could reinvigorate local politics, with local councils encouraging citizens to use the council website to participate directly in the decision-making process. A pilot scheme to gauge the potential of e-voting was used in the 2003 local elections.

The Scottish Parliament has set up two means by which the citizens of Scotland can use technology to contribute to decision making: the Scottish Parliament Discussion Forum, which has invited contributions on legislation such as the Licensing (Scotland) Bill; and 'seConsult', the electronic form of the formal consultation process.

Consultation

In what is a relatively recent development in participatory politics, UK government agencies have established small panels of citizens to offer advice on areas of policy. For example, in 2003 the Food Standards Agency established a 15-person jury to hear evidence about genetically modified (GM) food. After listening to representations from pressure groups and businesses, the jury recommended that GM foods should be available in the shops, but with warning stickers attached. The advice is not binding on the government, and is only part of a wider consultation exercise.

One of the interesting features of devolved politics in Scotland is the creation of an official consultation process. This is an opportunity for all citizens with an interest in a proposed area of Scottish Executive work to voice their opinion on whether and how the work should proceed. An example of this was the consultation on the structuring of tuition fees for residents of England and Wales who wanted to avoid paying 'top-up' fees by studying at universities in Scotland.

Central government, too, has picked up on the idea of consultation. In June 2005, it announced a consultation on the smoke-free (no smoking in public places and workplaces) elements of the Health Improvement and Protection Bill.

Task 1.2

What are the main advantages and disadvantages of direct democracy?

Guidance

The main advantages are as follows:

- It collapses the distinction between the governed and the government. In a direct democracy, the power of a minister is only that of an ordinary citizen when it comes to deciding if a measure will become law. Where initiatives are used, all citizens have the right to introduce proposed legislation.
- It increases the legitimacy of government decisions.
- It can lead to greater cooperation between different groups in society, and remove suspicion of elitism or prejudice.

Task 1.2 (continued)

- It might prevent campaigns of civil disobedience against new laws, as all citizens would have had the opportunity to decide on the law.

Direct democracy has been criticised for the following reasons:
- Results can be unfairly influenced by charismatic or wealthy individuals.
- It is impractical in a modern, industrialised society. Most issues are either too complex for voters to understand, or require a long period of time to get to grips with them. Most states are also simply too large to practise this form of democracy today.
- It could encourage the development of a 'tyranny of the majority' and ignore the interests of minority groups.
- It places decision making in the hands of the masses, who may be more influenced by short-term, selfish or populist concerns than an educated, professional group of politicians.

Representative democracy

This is a restrictive and partial form of democracy, as citizens only participate either at election time or via interest groups and do not exercise power on their own behalf. However, citizens can control the actions of the executive through regular elections.

The main issues surrounding the concept of **representation** have focused on the questions of who votes, how they vote and for what they vote. Scholars have also disagreed about how one person is supposed to represent another and what they actually represent. Table 1.2 outlines different theories of representation.

Table 1.2 Theories of representation

Model	Key points
Trustee model	Edmund Burke argued that MPs had a moral duty to take a long-term, national view of issues, and that constituents should have no control over them other than at election time.
Delegate model	MPs are nothing more than a mouthpiece for their constituents. As such, they must vote in parliament exactly according to constituents' wishes. MPs' own views on a matter are of little consequence.
Mandate model	MPs are not elected on their own merits but simply as representatives of a particular party. Once elected, they have a mandate to ensure that the party's manifesto is implemented. Therefore, they have to support their party at all times, unless it fails to deliver on its manifesto promises.

Learning point
Theories of representation
(a) What are the strengths and weaknesses of each theory of representation?
(b) Which theory best describes representation in the UK?

The most common form of **representative democracy** in the modern age is often referred to as **liberal democracy**.

The evolution of liberal democracy

Before the nineteenth century, the ideas of liberalism and democracy were felt to be incompatible. While liberals were content to limit executive power, they rejected any idea of popular sovereignty. Their reasons for doing so were varied:

- Those without property would simply vote the way of their landlords or bosses.
- The poor would endorse revolutionary ideas.
- Property was treated as an indication of political competence: in other words, by becoming economically independent, those who had property had proved their worth to society and therefore deserved the vote.

Towards the end of the eighteenth century, liberals began to challenge these views. Several thinkers influenced liberal ideas on democracy (see Box 1.2).

Box 1.2
Key liberal thinkers

Jean-Jacques Rousseau (1712–78)
'Man is born free; and everywhere he is in chains. One thinks himself the master of others, and still remains a greater slave than they.'

Thomas Paine (1737–1809)
'The principle of an equality of rights is clear and simple. Every man can understand it, and it is by understanding his rights that he learns his duties; for where the rights of man are equal, every man must, finally, see the necessity of protecting the rights of others, as the most effectual security for his own.'

John Stuart Mill (1806–73)
'It requires unusual moral courage as well as disinterestedness in a woman, to express opinions favourable to women's enfranchisement, until, at least, there is some prospect of obtaining it.'

As ideas about liberal democracy developed, it became possible to identify certain key principles:

- Government should be limited and its purpose should be the removal of obstacles to individual well-being.
- The market should play a major role and state interference in the economy should be minimal.
- The state should only play a 'night-watchman' role.
- The state should gradually be extended from men with property to members of the working class.
- Civil liberties should be protected through the 'rule of law'.
- There should be checks and balances within the political system.

What are the major forms of modern-day liberal democracy?

Twentieth-century liberal democracies have come to possess the following characteristics:

- They are representative democracies. Political authority is based on popular consent.
- Popular consent may be given by the whole adult population.
- Elections must be free and fair.
- Open competition must exist between individuals, groups and parties.

The two main ways in which liberal democracies work are through **parliamentary systems** and **presidential systems**.

Parliamentary systems

In parliamentary systems (see Figure 1.1), the leader of the government (the prime minister) holds his or her position by virtue of the fact that he or she is the leader of the largest party in parliament. He or she appoints the members of his or her government largely from the legislature. In the UK, the majority of ministers are elected Members of Parliament, and a relatively small number are appointed members of the House of Lords.

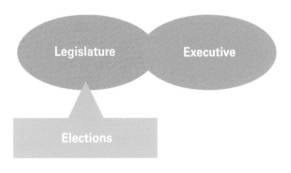

Figure 1.1 Parliamentary democracy

Merits of parliamentary systems

- The prime minister and his or her ministers are directly accountable to parliament for their actions. Weekly Prime Minister's Questions and regular Ministerial Questions enable MPs to scrutinise the actions of the executive. The government can be removed if it loses a motion of censure. The last time this happened in the UK was in 1979.
- Where a plurality system of election is used, such as first-past-the-post, it tends to deliver effective government as the winning party's share of seats is distorted due to the small size and large number of the constituencies. This results in the government enjoying a healthy majority over all of the other parties.

Weaknesses of parliamentary systems

- The distorting effect of a plurality electoral system leads to an imbalance in the relationship between the executive and legislature. Where MPs are expected to follow the party line closely, this can severely undermine both the independence of MPs and the accountability function of the legislature.
- Where a proportional system is used to elect MPs, parliamentary systems can lead to unstable government and political deadlock. Between 1945 and 2001, Italy experienced 59 different governments.

Presidential systems

Presidential systems differ from parliamentary systems in several ways, the most significant being the relationship between the executive and the legislature (see Figure 1.2). Whereas the institutions are entwined in a parliamentary system, presidential systems have a distinct separation of powers. The legislature has the power to reject presidential initiatives, and the president can veto legislative laws. This system of checks and balances is designed to prevent one institution dominating any of the others.

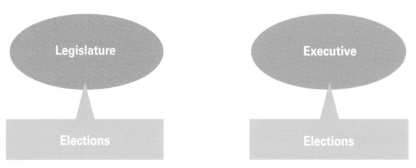

Figure 1.2 Presidential democracy

Merits of presidential systems

- Presidential systems prevent executive dominance, as the legislature has control over key areas of policy. In the USA this includes taxation and the right to declare war. The US Congress also has the power to remove a sitting president by impeaching him or her.
- It gives additional power to the citizen. Having the ability to balance the power of the legislature and the executive through separate elections gives the electorate greater choice. In 2001, George Bush lost control of the Senate to the Democrats. Similarly, French electors voted for a period of **cohabitation** in 1986–88, 1993–95 and 1997–2000.

Weaknesses of presidential systems

- The political system can become gridlocked due to two independent bodies trying separately to impose their own agenda. After the 1994 US mid-term elections, the Republicans took control of Congress and used this power to block President Clinton's attempts to get the budget passed.
- The role of the president is determined as much by cultural factors as by political ones. Reacting to the perceived abuse of presidential power in the war in southeast Asia, in the 1970s Congress determined to limit executive dominance in future. This took the form of legislation (War Powers Act 1974) and depriving the president of critical support in Congress.

How has the concept of liberal democracy been criticised?

Marxists criticise liberal democracy on the grounds that it is a smokescreen for the continued exploitation of the masses. They argue that it is an integral part of the capitalist system and is designed to give the impression of democracy while actually placing power in the hands of a wealthy elite. Voting is restricted to infrequent elections, and the range of policies in the political system is limited.

Some Conservatives have also levelled criticisms at UK liberal democracy. In 1976, Lord Hailsham described the UK system as an 'elective dictatorship'. He feared that the doctrine of parliamentary sovereignty threatened one of the pillars of the UK constitution: the 'rule of law'. Coupled with the distorting effect of the UK electoral system, this could effectively lead to one-party rule.

> The sovereignty of parliament has increasingly become, in practice, the sovereignty of the Commons, and the sovereignty of the Commons has increasingly become the sovereignty of the government which, in addition to its influence in government, controls the party whips, the party machine, and the civil service.
>
> Lord Hailsham, 21 October 1976

Elections

Liberal democracy relies on regular elections in order to provide popular consent. At a basic level, elections enable citizens to choose representatives to govern and legislate for them.

The central functions of elections depend on whether one takes a 'bottom-up' or 'top-down' view:

- The **bottom-up** view suggests that elections are a means by which politicians can be held accountable for their actions by the voters. Voters can therefore play a vital role in political recruitment and influencing policy. In countries such as the USA or France, the president is directly elected, thus giving the citizens a greater say in the composition of the government.
- The **top-down** view suggests that elections do not serve to hold politicians to account or influence policy, but actually strengthen elites and provide legitimacy for the actions of the ruling class. Radicals argue that elections fail to provide voters with real choice, as most of the parties comprise members with similar socioeconomic backgrounds and offer very similar policies.

How do elections function in practice?

This section explores how different types of electoral system operate, which will ultimately enable us to examine how effectively elections promote democracy.

Elections are held in the UK to elect representatives at local, regional, national and European levels. Until 1997, most people only ever got to vote using one type of electoral system. However, since then, the Labour government has introduced a range of new electoral systems as part of its constitutional reform package.

Most people over the age of 18 are entitled to vote. The only conditions are that they are a British or Commonwealth citizen, or a Republic of Ireland citizen living in the UK. In order to vote on polling day, you have to be included on the Electoral Register. Only the following groups of people are barred from voting: peers; convicted felons; anybody found guilty of election corruption within the last 5 years; and people who are suffering from a mental illness and are certified as being incapable of making a reasoned judgement. Voting is secret and voluntary.

The range of electoral systems can be divided into three categories:

- **plurality systems**, which simply require the winning candidate to gain more votes than the next most popular candidate
- **majoritarian systems**, in which the result produces a clear winner, who receives an overall majority of the total votes

- proportional systems, in which the number of seats a party receives more closely reflects the percentage of votes it received

Plurality systems

A **single member plurality** or **first-past-the-post** (FPTP) system is used for UK general elections and for local elections in England and Wales (not Northern Ireland or Scotland). The system is also used in the USA, Canada and India.

The system of electing MPs to the House of Commons has existed in its current format for a relatively short period of time. Until 1885, most constituencies elected several MPs — a practice that was only completely ended after the removal of 12 university seats in 1950.

There are currently 646 separate constituencies across the UK, each electing a single MP. In order to vote you simply put an 'X' next to the name of the candidate you support. The candidate who gets the most votes wins, regardless of whether or not he or she receives more than 50% support.

Once members have been individually elected, the party with the most seats in Parliament, regardless of whether or not it has a majority of the popular vote, becomes the next government.

Table 1.3 shows the result of the 2005 general election for the constituency of Middlesbrough South and East Cleveland. Mr A. Kumar was elected as MP for the constituency.

Table 1.3 Middlesbrough South and East Cleveland: general election, 2005

Candidate	Number of votes	% of votes
A. Kumar (Labour)	21,945	50.2
M. Brooks (Conservative)	13,945	31.9
C. Minns (Liberal Democrat)	6,049	13.8
G. Groves (BNP)	1,099	2.5
C. Bull (UKIP)	658	1.5

Majoritarian systems

Three examples of majoritarian systems are the **supplementary vote**, the **alternative vote** and the **second ballot system**.

Supplementary vote

The supplementary vote (SV) system was created by Labour MP Dale Campbell-Savours, and featured prominently in the Plant Report published by the Labour Party in 1993. As well as being used to elect the Mayor of

London and mayors in 12 English towns, a variant of it is used to elect the Sri Lankan president. In this case, the voter can express three preferences as opposed to two. The system also has much in common with the alternative vote (see page 17).

With the supplementary vote system, the voter is faced with two columns on the ballot paper. In the first column the first choice is indicated by marking an 'X', and in the second one the next preference is recorded in the same manner. Voters do not have to express a second preference if they do not wish to.

If one candidate gets 50% of the first preference vote, he or she is elected. In the short time in which this system has been used, this has been a rare occurrence. Only Robert Wales in Newham and Ray Mallon in Middlesbrough have managed this feat. If no candidate gains 50% of the vote, only the two most popular candidates go through to the next round, and the other candidates are eliminated. The second preferences of the eliminated candidates are then examined, and if they are for either of the two remaining candidates, their votes are transferred to those candidates. Whoever has the most votes at the end of the process wins. An example is given in Table 1.4.

Table 1.4   The result of the London mayoral election, 2004

Name	Party	First preference votes	Second preference votes	Result
K. Livingstone	Labour	685,541 (35.70%)	250,517 (13.04%)	Elected mayor
S. Norris	Conservative	542,423 (28.24%)	222,559 (11.59%)	
S. Hughes	Liberal Democrats	284,645		
F. Maloney	UKIP	115,665		
L. German	Respect	61,731		
J. Leppert	BNP	58,405		
D. Johnson	Green	57,331		
R. Gidoomal	Christian People's Alliance			
L. Reid	Independent Working Class Association			
T. Nagalingam	Independent candidate			
Turnout 1,920,533 (36.95%)				

Source: the Electoral Commission

Alternative vote

The alternative vote (AV) system is used to elect the Australian Lower House. It offers the voter the opportunity to place each of the candidates in rank order. Starting with the least popular, candidates are removed and their votes transferred until a winner with an absolute majority emerges. Voters are under no obligation to vote for more than their first choice.

Second ballot system

Under this twist of the supplementary vote, which is used in France, voters choose their preferred candidate, and if no candidate receives more than 50% of the vote, the leading candidates go forward to a second round of voting, usually held the following week.

Proportional systems

Proportional systems include the **single transferable vote**, the **closed list** and the **additional member system**.

Single transferable vote

The single transferable vote (STV) is used for local, assembly and European Parliament elections in Northern Ireland, and for local elections in Scotland. The region is divided into large multi-member constituencies, and each constituency elects between three and five representatives depending on its size. Voters can rank the candidates, putting a '1' for their favourite, a '2' for the next, and so on. They can also vote for just one candidate or accept the rank order of their preferred party.

In order to get elected, a candidate needs to receive a certain quota of votes. This quota (Q) is based on the formula:

$$Q = \frac{(\text{number of votes cast})}{(\text{number of seats in the constituency} + 1)} + 1$$

Once a candidate has gained the quota, any 'surplus' votes are transferred to the second-placed candidate and so on. This process is repeated each time someone gains sufficient votes to be elected. If a candidate receives insufficient first-preference votes and is eliminated, all the votes for that candidate are redistributed to the second-placed candidate on the ballot paper.

Closed list

There are many varieties of party list voting, but the most basic forms are the 'closed' and 'open' party list systems. Both systems require a multi-member constituency, which can, as with Israel, be a whole country.

Under the **open list** system, which is found in countries such as Belgium and the Netherlands, voters are free to choose between voting for an individual candidate and simply voting for their favourite party.

The **closed list** system is used for European Parliament elections in Great Britain. It is more straightforward than the open list, with voters only having the option to choose between the respective parties. After the votes have been counted, each party receives the same percentage of seats as votes received. Voters have advance knowledge of each party's rank order of candidates, and those candidates placed towards the top of their party's list stand a better chance of being elected than those lower down.

The European Parliament in Strasbourg

In the UK, there are 12 European electoral regions, with each region having between three and ten MEPs. Each group of MEPs is responsible for representing the whole of that region.

Additional member system

The additional member system (AMS) is used for the Scottish Parliament, Welsh Assembly and London Assembly elections. It is also used in Germany and New Zealand.

Several varieties of additional member system exist, but they are basically a combination of first-past-the-post and party list voting. The purpose is to retain the best features of FPTP while introducing proportionality between parties through party list voting.

The country is divided into several large electoral regions, containing a mixture of constituency and list seats. In Figure 1.3, the region has six seats: A–D represent the constituencies, and E and F are the list seats.

Each voter has two votes: one vote for a single MP via FPTP and one for a regional or national party list. The balance between the constituency and list seats varies between countries: in Germany and New Zealand there is a straight 50:50 split, but in Scotland it is 55:45 and Wales 67:33. There are different ways for election officers to work out how many seats a party should have won, but a commonly used method is as follows:

- Step 1: count the total number of votes cast and divide it by the number of constituency seats won in the region plus 1 (this is sometimes called a party's 'average').
- Step 2: the party with the highest figure receives the first 'top-up' seat. This is taken from the party list votes. If a party has been under-represented in the constituency vote, it is likely to receive more 'top-up' seats than a party that has benefited from the constituency vote.
- Step 3: the process is continued until all the 'top-up' seats in the region are filled. Each time a party receives a 'top-up' seat, its average changes. Usually, certain criteria have to be met before a party is eligible for a 'top-up' seat. In Germany, a party must win either 5% of the total vote or at least one constituency seat. In this way, it is hoped to prevent extremist parties with little concentrated support from gaining representation.

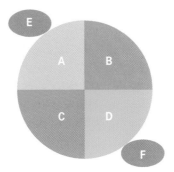

Figure 1.3 Additional member system

This system was introduced for the new regional assemblies in the UK after 1997. The Scottish Parliament is made up of 129 MSPs (Members of the Scottish Parliament). There are currently 73 constituency MSPs and 56 regional list MSPs.

The Welsh National Assembly consists of 60 elected members, elected from five electoral regions: 40 are constituency Assembly Members and are voted for using FPTP, while the remaining 20 are elected using a list system. In its review of the workings of AMS, the government's White Paper 'Better Governance for Wales' (June 2005) recommended that candidates be prevented from standing for election in both the constituency and list sections.

The London Assembly consists of 25 members elected from 14 constituencies. The remaining 11 members are known as 'London-wide members', as they are elected by votes cast across the whole of the Greater London Authority area and thus do not represent any particular constituency.

The mandate: how far do elections confer legitimacy on governments?

One of the central functions of elections is to fill positions of government. By receiving the endorsement of the electorate after a campaign in which their policies have been thoroughly scrutinised, governments can claim to have a legitimate right to implement their manifesto policies while in office. This is called a 'mandate to govern'. It can be argued that the doctrine of the mandate is of vital importance to any claim that elections contribute to democracy in the modern era. Without a mandate, there is little basis for elections to create a government 'of the people'.

The main arguments in defence of this theory are as follows:

- Voters tend to vote for a particular party as opposed to an individual.
- Voters are able to make an informed choice between the parties based on an awareness of their policy positions. Each party publishes a manifesto, whose contents are vigorously examined by critical media during the election campaign.

However, its relevance has been challenged:

- The mandate doctrine takes no account of changing circumstances and therefore denies the government sufficient flexibility.
- It is difficult to draw a direct link between voting and voter awareness of policy differences between the parties. There is some doubt among political analysts about the ability of voters to act rationally, that is, to examine the policies of each party and decide which ones best suit them. Indeed, there is plenty of evidence to suggest that wider factors such as social class, the media and the personality of party leaders has a greater impact on voting behaviour.
- The doctrine is difficult to apply to a coalition government as parties would probably have to compromise on elements of their manifesto as a part of a power-sharing deal. The idea of a mandate would therefore not exist in any country where a proportional electoral system was used.
- Parties deliberately keep their manifestos vague in an attempt to appeal to as wide a constituency as possible. They tend to concentrate on general values and beliefs instead of fully explained policies.
- The concept is further undermined by the distorting effect of FPTP. In 2005, the Labour government was elected with a 35.2% share of the vote, on a turnout of only 61%. Its mandate to govern therefore came from barely 25% of the electorate.

Conclusion: how effectively do elections promote democracy?

It is difficult to produce a definitive answer to this question. One of the chief reasons is that there is a wide range of electoral systems in use, each of them with differing effects.

Plurality systems, such as FPTP, do not require an overall majority, and thus cannot claim to represent the wishes of the country as a whole. This system has even, on two occasions, produced a government that did not achieve a simple majority of votes nationally, in 1951 and February 1974. In this sense, elections in the UK only serve to confirm the power of the elites and are not concerned with ensuring popular control of the government.

Even **proportional systems** struggle to assert their democratic credentials. As indicated above, they tend to produce coalition governments, whose survival is dependent on post-election deals being done behind closed doors. The fate of these governments can also rest on the whims of small coalition partners, such as the German FDP.

Elections also fail to perform a key democratic role as they are held so infrequently. Most liberal democratic states' primary claim to democratic status is their commitment to holding regular parliamentary or presidential elections. However, in the period between elections, the wishes of most citizens are ignored.

A more positive appraisal of the effectiveness of elections in contributing to democracy would begin by limiting the significance of democracy in a political system, identifying it purely as a means to choose who rules the state. This interpretation would obviously place elections as the primary instrument of democratic action.

Elections in liberal democracies also provide choice between competing ideas and personnel. While this choice is evidently greater in countries where 'open' proportional systems are in operation, even FPTP constituencies feature at least four candidates in competition.

Critically, elections give voters an opportunity to 'vote the rascals out'. In this case, FPTP has distinct advantages over rival systems, as the nature of the government is determined by the electorate, not by party elites.

The development of modern society has made it impossible for direct democracy to function effectively. For over 100 years, liberal democracies have therefore relied on elections as the next best thing. However, a combination of voter disillusionment with mainstream political parties and the development

of more direct forms of communication have meant that the dominance of **representative democracy** could be under serious threat.

Task 1.3

(a) In what ways do elections contribute to democracy?

(b) Using Table 1.3 and your own knowledge, assess how effective elections are in contributing to democracy in the UK.

Guidance

(a) Include the following points: elections provide choice between candidates and parties; they enable citizens to choose their representatives and rulers, and vote them out if necessary; they are a practical way of meeting the challenge of selecting representatives in a modern, industrialised society.

(b) The structure of your answer is essential when tackling this question. Try to think about the criteria that you would use to analyse elections. These might include accountability, fair representation of popular opinion, frequency of elections, mandates. The winner of Middlesbrough South and East Cleveland can claim to have a mandate, as he has been supported by over half the constituency. This, however, is in itself a rarity in UK general elections; many MPs struggle to get more than 40% of the popular vote. He is also accountable to them for his actions, as he knows that he will have to face them again within 5 years. However, within that time period he is likely to be guided more by the interests of his party than by those of his constituents, and the voters can do very little about this until the next general election comes around.

Useful websites

- The Administration and Cost of Elections Project
  www.aceproject.org/main/english/index.htm
- The Boundary Commission for England
  www.statistics.gov.uk/pbc
- Direct Democracy in Switzerland
  www.swissworld.org/dvd_rom/eng/direct_democracy_2004/index.html

Further reading

- Garnett, M. (2005) 'Is the UK a liberal democracy?', *Politics Review*, vol. 15, no. 2.
- Heywood, A. (2000) *Key Concepts in Politics*, Palgrave Macmillan.

Does the current method of electing MPs need replacing?

The debate over first-past-the-post

According to supporters of FPTP, one of the system's virtues is the fact that it has proved durable and effective over a long period of time. However, it is arguably only due to reforms of the system during the last 150 years that it has survived at all. For example, until 1885, most constituencies elected several MPs — a practice that was only completely ended after the removal of the 12 university seats in 1950. All 12 of these MPs were elected not under FPTP, but under the single transferable vote (STV).

The debate over the continued merits of FPTP is not a new one. For example, the 1917 all-party Speaker's Conference recommended a switch to STV in the towns and to AV (alternative vote) in the counties. However, many of the arguments surrounding the continued use of FPTP for general elections have remained the same during the last few decades.

What are the main arguments in favour of reforming the current system for electing MPs?

The principal arguments in favour of **electoral reform** are as follows:

- The party that wins a majority of the seats in parliament rarely wins an over-all majority of votes cast (see Figure 2.1).
- The percentage vote that a party receives is not accurately reflected in its percentage share of the seats in the House of Commons. For example, 35% of the electorate voted for Labour in 2005, yet it received 55% of the seats. This is a **deviation from proportionality** (DV) of +20. Labour actually received fewer votes than in 1979 — an election that the party lost.

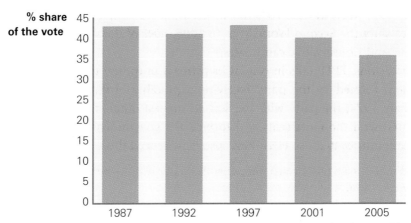

Figure 2.1 Winning party's share of the vote in general elections, 1987–2005

- By way of contrast, smaller parties tend to lose out under FPTP. In 2005, the Liberal Democrats gained only 9% of the seats even after gaining 22% of the votes — a DV of –13.
- In the last three general elections, the electoral system has been biased in favour of Labour. Historically, both main parties have benefited more or less equally from the distorting effect of FPTP, but since 1997 it has clearly worked for Labour (see Box 2.1). As a consequence, some academics believe that the Conservatives would have required 43% of the vote to have won an overall majority in 2001, while Labour would have required only 36%. In 2005, there was only 2.9% difference in their share of the popular vote, yet Labour enjoyed a massive 25% advantage in the number of seats won.
- The system tends to favour large parties that enjoy support which is evenly spread throughout the country. One factor that has contributed to Labour's electoral dominance since 1997 is the party's ability to win seats throughout the UK. By contrast, Scotland and Wales have been virtual electoral deserts for the Conservative Party, while the Liberal Democrats have traditionally found it difficult to win seats in Wales, the South East and the North East.
- FPTP tends to support a two-party system. No other party has held office apart from Labour and Conservative

Box 2.1

Factors that swing the system Labour's way

- Labour-held seats tend to have fewer constituents than Conservative-held seats; therefore require fewer voters to win a seat.
- Voters are increasingly prepared to vote tactically and negatively to keep their most disliked party out. Historically, this has hit the Conservatives hardest, with Labour voters switching to the Liberal Democrats either to unseat Conservatives or to keep them out.

since 1929, while at least 70% of the electorate has voted for the two main parties since the Second World War. In 2005, 80% of the seats were won by Labour and Conservative candidates.

- On occasions, FPTP fails in one of its primary purposes: to produce a government formed by the party receiving a plurality of votes. In 1951 and February 1974, the party with the second highest number of votes was the one that won the most seats and formed the government (see Table 2.1). Other countries that use FPTP have also experienced this.

Table 2.1 Winner takes all? Occasions when the party with a plurality of votes did not win the most seats

Election	Country	% votes		% seats
1951	UK	Labour	48.8	47.20
		Conservative	48	51.36
1974 (Feb)	UK	Labour	37.2	47.40
		Conservative	37.8	46.77
1981	New Zealand	National Party	47.0	38.8
		Labour	43.0	39.0

What are the arguments in favour of retaining the existing system?

Despite its disadvantages, several arguments can be made in favour of FPTP:

- It is easy to understand and operate. A single 'X' by the name of the preferred candidate is sufficient to indicate your choice. The number of crosses is added up and the result is obtained — usually within a few hours of the polling stations closing. Since 1992, Sunderland South has delivered its result faster than any other constituency, and by 2005 it had refined its counting procedures to the extent that it was able to announce the result at 10.41 p.m., just 41 minutes after the polls had closed.
- It has stood the test of time. It has arguably been the mainstay of our moderate, evolutionary political culture, and compares favourably with the experience of other countries in Europe that have experimented with different systems.
- FPTP generally secures strong and stable government. Each of the governments elected since October 1974 has been able to last at least 4 years without the need for a further general election. All but two of those governments have also enjoyed a very comfortable majority in the House of Commons. This has made it easier for them to carry out their manifesto promises.

MPs sitting in the House of Commons

- Conversely, FPTP makes it relatively easy to get rid of unpopular govern-ments. As the elections of 1979 and 1997 demonstrate, the two-party system enables voters to switch allegiances if they want to replace the governing party with an alternative. By way of comparison, governments elected under proportional representation (PR) are more often than not removed by one or more coalition partners switching allegiances rather than as a result of changes in voter preference.

- Defenders of the system point to the strong links that exist between an MP and his or her constituency. Voters know the identity of each candidate and in most cases have contributed to the selection process. Constituents can therefore contact their MP directly should they wish to raise a particular issue. Most importantly, they can hold their own MP to account for his or her record in parliament at the next general election, and, if necessary, vote him or her out.

- FPTP encourages political moderation, as parties know that they have to maintain a broad appeal to win elections. This not only discourages the formation of extremist parties, but also allows more independently minded figures to find a home in the major parties, where their political extravagances can be safely indulged.

- It has allowed both major political parties an even share of power. During the last 16 elections, the Conservatives narrowly shade Labour in terms of election victories.

The alternatives to first-past-the-post

Having explored the workings of each system in the previous chapter, it is necessary to examine their effects if we are to discover a viable alternative to FPTP.

Majoritarian systems

Supplementary vote

The SV system has the following effects:

- The overall winner can claim to have won the support of the broad majority of voters.
- In order to achieve this, parties have to reach out to a broad spectrum of voters.
- However, it is rare for a candidate to achieve an overall majority of votes in the first round, and he or she may even struggle to gain sufficient second-preference votes to gain an overall majority.
- Votes can be 'wasted' if people don't vote for either of the two most popular candidates as first or second preferences.
- Critics of SV argue that it is too complicated for some voters to understand, and therefore results in a significant number of unintentionally spoiled ballot papers. In the October 2005 mayoral election in Torbay, 1,750 of 24,500 ballot papers issued were spoiled. According to the Electoral Reform Society, this was either through a failure to understand the system, or because some voters did not nominate a second-preference candidate.

Alternative vote

The main effects of the AV system are as follows:

- It encourages voters to cross party lines and base their preferences on the personalities of the various candidates. In the process, it offers voters a greater choice of candidates: in the UK, voters would not be forced to choose between expressing their genuine ideological preference, on the one hand, and exercising a realistic vote according to the situation in their particular constituency, on the other.
- Critics of the system argue that it leads to an over-representation of centre parties because they are often the second choice of most voters. This could lead to one party suffering disproportionately if it is not popular with the voters. If AV had been used in 1997 and 2001, the Conservatives would have received even fewer seats than they did under FPTP.

• In his submission to the Independent Commission on the Voting System (also known as the Jenkins Commission), David Butler argued that AV had too much potential to produce a random result. He pointed out that the result in a constituency could depend not on who gets the highest number of first-preference votes, but on which party came second. To illustrate this, consider the example in Table 2.2, where in the first scenario the Liberal Democrat candidate finishes third and distribution of the Liberal Democrats' second preferences results in a win for the Conservative, who also topped the first-preference vote. However, if the positions of the Labour and Liberal Democrat candidates are reversed (scenario 2), and the Labour preferences favour the Liberal Democrat 20–9, then the Liberal Democrat wins.

Table 2.2 Potential randomness in the AV system

Party	First-preference votes (%)	Second-preference votes (%)	Result (%)
Scenario 1			
Conservative	40	14	54
Labour	31	15	46
Liberal Democrat	29		
Scenario 2			
Conservative	40	9	49
Liberal Democrat	31	20	51
Labour	29		

• AV can benefit candidates placed at the top of the ballot paper. In response to the profusion of candidates standing in each constituency, some voters have resorted to numbering the candidates 1 to 10 (or whatever is the number of candidates on the ballot paper) from top to bottom. This is known as the 'donkey vote' (see Box 2.2).

Box 2.2

The donkey vote

In Australian elections, it is estimated that the donkey vote makes up 2% of the total vote. Until 1984, this had a partial impact on the final result as candidates were listed alphabetically, so parties might have benefited by selecting candidates whose surnames began with letters at the start of the alphabet.

- Like other majoritarian systems, AV can penalise smaller parties. Under simulations of the 1992 general election, the Liberal Democrats in the UK would have won only 4.8% of the seats; in Australia, the Democratic Labor Party and the Democrats have never won a seat under AV.

Second ballot system

The effects of the second ballot system are as follows:
- The winning candidate can claim majority support.
- It allows voters to reconsider their original choices, if necessary.
- It creates strong and stable government.
- Critics argue that it restricts choice in the second round. In the 2002 French presidential election, left-wing voters were faced in the second round with a choice between the conservative Jacques Chirac and the National Front leader, Jean-Marie Le Pen.

Proportional systems

Single transferable vote

The STV system has the following effects:
- There are far fewer wasted votes, as most of the votes ultimately help elect a candidate.
- In common with most forms of PR, STV usually leads to greater diversity among elected representatives. As this system allows voters to place candidates in rank order, for example, they can express a clear preference for a woman candidate, should they want to see more women in the legislature. Equally, they could use the rank order to increase the likelihood of minority parties gaining representation.
- It generally results in a multi-party system, where there is an average of five parties winning more than 3% of the seats each.
- It can result in a different kind of politics being practised, with closer co-operation between parties before and after the election. During the 1998 Northern Ireland Assembly elections, the SDLP encouraged its supporters to deploy their second-preference votes in favour of parties that supported the Good Friday Agreement.
- While the voting is reasonably straightforward, the counting process is complicated and can take a long time. This is one of the reasons why STV is found only in countries with relatively small populations, such as Australia (the Senate), Malta and the Republic of Ireland.

- The need to secure a high ranking can lead to infighting between candidates from the same party, and elected representatives giving undue attention to local issues, at the expense of national considerations.

Closed list

The effects of closed list PR are as follows:

- The most obvious one is that a greater number of parties are able to win seats. Compared to FPTP, which averages around three parties winning over 3% of the seats, in list systems almost five parties are able to achieve this total. Of the 78 UK seats available at the 2004 European Parliament election, UKIP was able to win 12 seats and the Greens won two.
- As this is the purest form of PR, it features many of the general advantages of other proportional systems. Therefore, voting tends to be fairer and there are fewer 'wasted' votes.

Additional member system

AMS has the following effects:

- One of its advantages is that it offers greater voter choice. By 'splitting the ticket', voters can select a different party for their constituency and list votes. However, as Table 2.3 illustrates, the extent to which voters take full advantage of this opportunity is surprisingly limited.

Table 2.3 Split-ticket voting in Scotland, Wales, Germany and New Zealand

Election	% ticket splitters
Scotland 1999	20
Scotland 2003	28
Wales 1999	23
Wales 2003	17
London 2000	21
Germany 1998	23
Germany 2002	20
New Zealand 1999	35
New Zealand 2002	37

Source: ICPR, *Changed Voting Changed Politics: Lessons of Britain's Experience of PR since 1997 — Final Report of the Independent Commission to Review Britain's Experience of PR Voting Systems*, The Constitution Unit (2003).

- AMS generally increases the number of parties gaining representation. The 2003 elections to the Scottish Parliament illustrate this perfectly (see Table 2.4). In total there are nine parties with Members of the Scottish Parliament (MSPs), a figure that includes two independents and five parties that are not represented at Westminster.

Table 2.4 Scottish Parliament election, 1 May 2003 (turnout: 49.4%)

Party	% of constituency vote	No. of FPP seats	% of FPP seats	% of regional vote	No. of regional seats	Total no. of seats	% of total no. of seats
Con	16.8	3	4.1	15.5	15	18	14.0
Labour	35.1	46	63.0	29.3	4	50	38.8
Lib Dem	15.6	13	17.8	11.8	4	17	13.2
SNP	24.1	9	12.3	20.9	18	27	20.9
Green	—	—	—	6.9	7	7	5.4
SSP	6.3	—	—	6.7	6	6	4.7
Others	3.5	2	2.7	8.7	2	4	3.1
Total	100	73	100	100	56	129	100

Source: the Electoral Commission

- It has also led to greater representation of women. The Welsh Assembly became the first legislature in the world to have 50% women members after the elections in 2003.
- From a governing point of view, the proportional nature of AMS invariably leads to coalitions having to be formed. In Scotland, Labour holds power with the Liberal Democrats, while in Germany the SPD shares power with the Greens. However, the need to share power depends entirely on the balance between the number of constituency and list seats. Where there is a significant bias towards constituency seats, as is the case in Wales, it is more likely that a party can govern alone. After the 2003 Welsh Assembly elections, Labour decided it could do without a coalition partner as it had won 50% of the assembly seats.
- This can also be considered a criticism of AMS, as it gives disproportionate power to smaller coalition partners. This is best illustrated by reference to the behaviour of the FDP in Germany. Despite averaging approximately 9.5% of the vote, it remained in office from 1969 until 1998, holding three or four cabinet posts in the process. It was also responsible for the fall of the SPD administration in 1982, when it decided that it would transfer its loyalties to the conservative CDU/CSU.

Task 2.1

'The main problem with AMS is that it combines the weaknesses of FPTP with the flaws of list PR.' Discuss.

Guidance

To agree with the statement, you could use the following arguments:

- In the German model, half the MPs are not directly accountable to the electorate.
- These same list MPs are thus dependent on the party leadership for their place on the list. This increases the power of the party leadership.
- Meanwhile, the constituency MPs fail to represent their whole constituency because they rarely gain an overall majority of the vote.
- AMS leads to a long delay in the formation of the government and can increase the power of behind-the-scenes elites after the election. Some reference to the interparty manoeuvrings after the 2005 German election would be useful.

To challenge the statement, you should demonstrate the strengths of the system:

- The use of two electoral systems allows one to compensate for the other's weaknesses. Where list systems fail to provide a strong constituency link, the FPTP element provides for that perfectly. Whereas FPTP has a natural distorting effect, the list votes act as a 'top-up' for parties that have not been fairly represented by the constituency votes.
- While AMS is normally 100% proportional in Germany, it has also produced the type of stable governments that are the hallmark of political systems where FPTP is used.
- AMS increases voter choice, as voters can differentiate between the constituency and list contests and, if so inclined, 'split the ticket'.

Attitude of the parties and the public towards reform of the system

Labour Party

Historically, the Labour Party has been sceptical about the issue of electoral reform. Believing that FPTP worked to its advantage, the party paid little attention to it until the late 1980s when the Labour Campaign for Electoral Reform received a surge in support. After a fourth successive general election defeat in 1992, the party leadership commissioned Lord Plant to investigate alternatives to FPTP for general elections and the elections that would accompany the party's proposed constitutional changes. Although his recommendations were not wholly adopted by the party leadership, his commission did provide an ideological impetus to the campaign for reform among Labour Party members.

Learning point

Plant Report

The recommendations of the Plant Commission included:
- general elections: supplementary vote
- European Parliament: regional list
- House of Lords: regional list

Why were these particular systems recommended for the different elections?

It was not until the election of Tony Blair that supporters of reform got the breakthrough they wanted, as he included a promise in Labour's 1997 manifesto to introduce a commission to investigate alternatives to FPTP, and to hold a referendum on the issue within the lifetime of that parliament.

The multi-party commission, under the chairmanship of Lord Jenkins of Hillhead, eventually recommended replacing FPTP with a completely original electoral system. Influenced by the popularity of mixed systems among countries adopting new electoral systems — such as New Zealand and Japan — the commission created a variant of AMS called alternative vote plus (AV+).

In order to achieve fairer representation and a more proportional result, between 15 and 20% of MPs would be elected by list PR. These would be the top-up representatives from the regions. However, stable government and a strong MP–constituency link would be maintained by the majority of MPs being elected from single-member constituencies using the alternative vote. Figure 2.2 shows how the use of Jenkins's system would have changed the result of the 2005 general election, and Figure 2.3 shows what an AV+ ballot paper might look like.

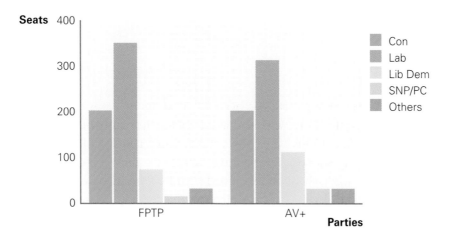

Figure 2.2 How using AV+ would have affected the general election of 2005

Constituency vote

This vote will help to decide who the constituency MP for Hoggborough East is. Rank the candidates in order of preference (1 for your preferred candidate, then 2, 3 etc.). Rank as many candidates as you wish.

Regional vote

This vote will help to decide the total number of seats for each party in the county of Rochefolk. You may vote either for one party or for one of the listed candidates. A vote for a listed candidate will also be counted as a vote for that candidate's party.

EITHER
Put an X by the party of your choice
OR
Put an X by the candidate of your choice

Sam Beard
Liberal Democrat

- ☐ **Liberal Democrat**
- ☐ Alison Marks
- ☐ Barry Russell
- ☐ Marie White

Stephen Blake
Green

- ☐ **Green**
- ☐ Malcolm Goate
- ☐ Louise Jones
- ☐ Alice Smith

Rebecca Nuttall
Conservative

- ☐ **Conservative**
- ☐ Peter Fox
- ☐ Akhil Kara
- ☐ Jo Nell

Bruce Oute
UKIP

- ☐ **UKIP**
- ☐ Peter Boss
- ☐ Richard Charles
- ☐ Ian Lacey

Lyn Wheen
Labour

- ☐ **Labour**
- ☐ Monica Aluwahlia
- ☐ Olive Bear
- ☐ Tom Bernard

Henry Kiernan
Independent

Figure 2.3 How an AV+ ballot paper might look

The government's response to the Jenkins Report was lukewarm. The prime minister expressed his approval of the hard work and thought that had gone into the process, but he did not endorse the proposed system itself. Tellingly, the official response of the government was provided by the home secretary, Jack Straw, a renowned opponent of PR, who was not slow to voice his own scepticism about any alternative to FPTP.

Two general elections later, no referendum on the method of electing representatives to Westminster has yet been held. Several reasons have been put forward for this:

- Blair was never really interested in electoral reform in the first place: it was a legacy of John Smith's period as Labour Party leader. Sceptics claim that Blair only agreed to look at the issue again when he thought that he might need to form a coalition with the Liberal Democrats after the 1997 election.
- The success of Labour in the last three general elections has restored the party's faith in FPTP.
- Meanwhile, Labour's experience of PR in London, Welsh, Scottish and European elections has not been a happy one.
- In order to support reform publicly, Blair would need the support of his cabinet and his MPs. There is little evidence to suggest that there is majority support for PR in either cabinet or parliament.

Conservative Party

Given Tory hostility to most aspects of constitutional reform, it should be no surprise to discover that the Conservatives oppose any move away from FPTP. Like Labour, they believe that FPTP works in their favour, with periods out of office being more than matched by the number of times that the system has secured them power. They also reject reform on the grounds that it leads to weak and unstable coalition governments, which depend heavily on the acquiescence of minor coalition partners.

> Proportional representation prevents voters from kicking out an unpopular government and leads to extremist and minority parties being elected with as little as 5% of the vote.
>> Oliver Heald, Shadow Secretary of State for Constitutional Affairs, June 2005

In its contribution to the debate on the workings of FPTP after the 2005 election, the party emphasised its resistance to reform, relying instead on calling for fixed-size constituencies to prevent the discrepancy in value between Conservative and Labour votes recurring.

The Conservatives also strongly support the view of Michael Pinto-Duschinsky that a prime function of an electoral system is to give the voters the means to remove an ineffective government. Pinto-Duschinsky argues that FPTP performs this role better than any other variant. Boris Johnson agrees:

> I say: to hell with PR, long live first-past-the-post, and safeguard, for the people, the right to kick into outer space a government they dislike.
>> Boris Johnson, Conservative MP

Boris Johnson, Conservative MP

However, there are periods when prominent members of the party have advocated replacing FPTP. After the two election defeats of 1974, the Conservative Action for Electoral Reform was established, including such luminaries as Douglas Hurd and Chris Patten as members. The return of a Conservative government in 1979, however, diminished the group's impact. It remains to be seen whether the success of the Conservatives in PR elections since 1997, and their failure to win power under FPTP since that date, will prompt a radical rethink in the party's approach to the issue.

In the aftermath of the 2005 defeat, the Electoral Reform Society published a pamphlet entitled 'The Conservatives and the Electoral System', which made a strong case for the Conservatives to embrace the cause of electoral reform. It failed to make an impact on either of the two contenders for the party leadership, however, and the prospect of change in the near future looks slim.

Task 2.2

In the light of three successive general election defeats, do you agree with the view that the Conservatives should look more favourably at electoral reform?

Guidance

Arguments that suggest the Conservatives should look favourably at reform might include:

- In each of the last three elections, the system has been biased against them. It is estimated that, even if they and Labour had polled 33.8% in 2005, Labour would still have obtained over 100 seats more than them.
- A future Conservative victory could be prevented by the kind of **tactical voting** that cost them seats in 1997 and 2001. This would be more difficult to do under PR.
- Labour's share of the vote was artificially depressed in the last two elections due to low turnout among its traditional voters. They might be more inclined to vote in a close contest in order to prevent a Conservative victory.
- In elections where some form of PR has been used in the UK, the Conservatives have performed creditably; they even 'won' the 2004 European Parliament elections.

Arguments that suggest they should reject the idea might include:

- The party most likely to benefit from electoral reform is the Liberal Democrats, who might be more inclined to work in government with Labour than the Conservatives.

- PR would actually see the Conservatives shed voters to right-wing minor parties such as UKIP and the BNP, or even the Liberal Democrats. It might also see the emergence of a breakaway pro/anti-European party, which would also take votes away from the Conservatives.
- Historically, FPTP has served the party well, and will do so again in future. The wave of anti-Conservative tactical voting appeared to subside in 2005, and Labour's majority was severely dented in the 2005 election.

Liberal Democrat Party

The Liberal Democrats have had the longest commitment to PR of all the major parties, with a sustained advocacy of the merits of STV since the nineteenth century. In their eyes, it offers greater voter choice and ensures the fairest result. Their position can be explained partially by self-interest — FPTP has done them no favours since the First World War — but their belief in the role of the individual, and limiting the power of elites, also makes STV appear a more attractive proposition.

Learning point

Liberal Democrats and electoral reform

Liberal Democrat leader Charles Kennedy wrote to the prime minister on 25 May 2005 on the topic of electoral reform:

I have repeatedly made clear that I would welcome constructive engagement with any serious political party about introducing proportional representation. I believe it would strengthen our democracy by making parliament more directly accountable to individual voters. A government elected by proportional representation would have a clearer and more authoritative mandate. Tactical voting would become a thing of the past.

(a) Would a government elected under PR enjoy a greater mandate?

(b) How would tactical voting become 'a thing of the past'?

Minor parties

Most of the prominent minor parties support reform of the electoral system. The Greens advocate the introduction of AMS, while at the last election the SNP and Plaid Cymru argued for a more proportional system. Even an apparently conservative party such as UKIP also follows this line, highlighting its success under the regional list system used for European Parliament elections as one reason for its rejection of FPTP.

Public opinion

Opponents of reform often dismiss the issue as something that the majority of the population have little interest in and even less knowledge about. What most voters are concerned about, they argue, is whether the government that is returned after an election is both strong and stable.

To an extent, opinion poll evidence supports this view, with relatively few people expressing support for the introduction of PR in polls conducted between 1992 and 2003. Indeed, in an NOP poll conducted for *The Independent* in May 2005, 57% of respondents expressed support for the view that 'It is right that Labour have an overall majority because they won more votes than anyone else'.

However, in the same poll, 62% of people stated that they supported the introduction of a proportional system of electing MPs. This figure corroborates the views of some academics who argue that people's own experience of elections has a direct impact on their attitude to electoral systems. For example, levels of support for the use of AMS are far higher in Scotland, where it has been used for elections to the Scottish Parliament, than in England, which has had no such experience, and has therefore not had the opportunity to enjoy the benefits of PR.

Conclusion: is reform of the electoral system desirable?

It is almost impossible to provide an objective response to this question. The answer one could provide depends entirely on the criteria being deployed to make a judgement. The Jenkins Commission was provided with four specific criteria upon which to reach its verdict. They were:

- maintenance of the constituency link
- broad proportionality
- voter choice
- stable government

If we take recent electoral history as a guide, FPTP still successfully performs its core function of electing a stable government, while maintaining a strong MP–constituency link. Even with under 25% of the electorate voting for the Labour Party, few people seriously questioned its right to form a government after the 2005 election.

However, as previously stated, FPTP fails either to deliver broad proportionality or to provide real voter choice. Previously, neither of these points would have attracted much attention, but with the system so clearly working to

Labour's advantage on a consistent basis, and with a steady increase in the number of parties enjoying electoral success under other systems in the UK, a growing number of people are starting to question the suitability of FPTP for Westminster elections.

But what are the chances of FPTP being replaced in the near future? Politicians of all parties are aware of the fact that electoral systems, like constitutions, are not neutral. They are designed to serve a specific purpose, usually that of the party which designed them. While Labour continues to gain such clear advantages from FPTP, it is unlikely to ditch a system that has served it so well since 1997. The likelihood of reform in the near future, therefore, is undoubtedly slim. Although newspapers such as *The Independent* have launched an energetic campaign to galvanise interest and support for PR, the leaderships of both major parties are implacably wedded to FPTP.

While not publicly participating in the debate since the election, Tony Blair has allowed the deputy prime minister, John Prescott, and Lord Falconer to act as his mouthpieces. Both have offered a clear rejection of any move to implement Labour's 1997 manifesto pledge to hold a referendum on the system used for general elections. For the moment, then, the prospect of electoral reform in the UK remains hidden in the long grass.

Task 2.3

As a result of last week's election, demands for proportional representation to be used for electing MPs — just as it is, in one way or another, for Euro MPs, members of the Scottish Parliament or Welsh Assembly, or even mayors — are once again rustling the political undergrowth. Two newspapers have come out in favour of it, and at the weekend a member of the original Jenkins Commission that looked into the whole question of voting systems back in 1997–98 was even to be heard denouncing last week's general election as 'a travesty of democracy'. According to the Labour peer Lord Lipsey, it is high time the Tories woke up to just how far the present system of electing MPs is 'viciously biased' against them.

The Times, 10 May 2005

(a) What do you understand by the term 'electoral reform'?

(b) Outline a case for reforming the electoral system used for general elections in the UK.

Guidance

(a) Refer to a movement that aims to change the mechanism by which people vote in elections. Perhaps include examples of the perceived flaws of FPTP and a group that supports reform, such as the Electoral Reform Society.

Task 2.3 (continued)

Guidance

(b) Remember to make your points clear and precise. Where possible, provide a relevant recent example to illustrate your argument. Make sure that you are familiar with how the 2005 general election strengthened the case for reform. Your range of arguments should include the following observations:

- The system is heavily biased in favour of the Labour Party.
- It under-represents minority interests such as the Greens.
- No government since the Second World War has obtained an overall majority of votes, yet the system creates an 'elective dictatorship' that allows the governing party to do as it pleases.
- Even though it polled only 3% less than Labour in 2005, the Conservative Party will need to increase its share of the vote by at least 11% simply to win an overall Commons majority at the next election.
- Not all votes are equal — most elections are really decided by the preferences of about 1 million voters living in marginal seats.

Useful websites

- The Electoral Reform Society
  www.electoral-reform.org.uk/
- The Electoral Commission
  www.electoralcommission.org.uk
- Make Votes Count
  www.makemyvotecount.org.uk
- Electoral Reform Coalition New Zealand
  www.mmp.org.nz

Further reading

- Denver, D. (2003) 'Whatever happened to electoral reform?' *Politics Review*, vol. 13, no. 1.
- Electoral Reform Society (2005) 'The Conservatives and the Electoral System'.

What factors influence the way people vote?

One of the attractions of studying voting behaviour, or **psephology**, is that it focuses on how and why ordinary people interact with the political process. What is it that prompts someone to place their cross next to the name of a particular candidate? In the pre-democratic age — that is, until the introduction of the mass franchise and, crucially, the secret ballot in 1872 — the answer to this question would have been a lot simpler. Bribery, fear and alcoholic inducements would all have played a significant part in explaining election results.

However, as political parties and the electorate grew in tandem, it became considerably more difficult to explain away the fortunes of parties at general elections. What is surprising, therefore, is that the first major academic study of voting behaviour was not published until shortly after the Second World War. Since that time, various theories or **models** of voting behaviour have been put forward. This chapter explains each of the main theories in turn, and evaluates critically how relevant they are in explaining both why individuals vote in the way they do, and the results of recent general elections.

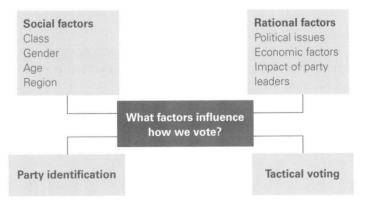

Figure 3.1 Factors affecting voting behaviour

How far do social factors influence voting behaviour?

The earliest studies of how people voted all highlighted the importance of particular social characteristics in influencing the voter's actions at the ballot box. That is to say, people identified themselves with a particular social group, and voted for the party that they felt was best able to meet the demands of that group. Although this behaviour is difficult to analyse accurately, academics were led to conclude that voters saw themselves as part of a group, and were either able to recognise common group interests or sufficiently influenced by their family members, workmates etc. to vote in a certain direction.

> A person thinks, politically, as he is socially. Social characteristics determine political preference.
> P. Lazarsfeld, B. Berelson and H. Gaudet, *The People's Choice* (1944)

A person's class, age, religion or gender therefore all had a strong influence. However, most studies until the mid-1970s emphasised the importance of **class** as the most significant social influence on voting.

Class

The era of alignment

The starting point for any explanation of the role of class in influencing voting behaviour has to be Butler and Stokes's classic work, *Political Change in Britain* (1969). This laid down an analysis that is the basis of all argument on how people vote.

The core of their argument is as follows:

- Voters can identify one party as representing the interests of a particular class (Labour for the working class and the Conservatives for the middle class).
- Voters do not believe that 'their' party is necessarily hostile to other classes; in other words, by voting for that party they believe that they are acting in the much broader national interest.
- Loyalty to that party does not automatically originate from approval for that party's policies, merely from a belief that this is what someone from that class should do. Thus, a welder from the northeast might vote Labour because that is what most other manual workers from that region do.
- Voters are significantly influenced by their parents and their peers (a process known as **socialisation**) into supporting one party, and align themselves with this party for most of their lifetime. This process of party identification is dealt with in greater detail later in the chapter.

At the time there was ample evidence to support Butler and Stokes's viewpoint. The UK had a strong two-party system, with little political instability. In an era of relatively low social mobility, both Labour and Conservative parties dominated UK politics and enjoyed a roughly equal share of power between 1945 and 1979. As Table 3.1 demonstrates, there was considerable statistical evidence to support Butler and Stokes's argument.

Table 3.1 Occupational class of 'head of household' and party choice, 1964–70

Party	1964 (%)		1966 (%)		1970 (%)	
	Non-manual	Manual	Non-manual	Manual	Non-manual	Manual
Con	62	28	61	25	63	33
Lab	22	64	26	69	26	58
Lib Dem	15	8	13	5	9	7
Other	—	0	0	—	2	2

Source: British Election Study 1964–70, reproduced from D. Denver, *Elections and Voters in Britain* (2003).

How relevant is this argument in the modern political age? As will be demonstrated later, Butler and Stokes's model has been exposed to some harsh criticism. However, the evidence from the last two general elections offers some support to the view that class is still an influential determinant of electoral behaviour, even if it can probably no longer be viewed as the single most influential factor.

Learning point
How do you determine class?
Several different ways have been attempted to determine the class to which people belong. The two most commonly used are, first, the '6-point scale':
- A Higher professional, managerial and administrative
- B Intermediate professional, managerial and administrative
- C1 Supervisory, clerical and other non-manual
- C2 Skilled manual
- D Semi-skilled and unskilled manual
- E Residual, casual workers, people reliant on state benefits

and, second, the broader distinction between 'manual' and non-manual' workers.

What are the advantages and disadvantages of defining class in these ways?

How has the class-based approach to explaining voting behaviour been criticised?

The class-based approach to explaining voting behaviour has been criticised in several ways:

- A significant amount of 'cross-class' voting took place, even during the high-point of the two-party system. This explains partially why the Conservatives were able to hold power in 1951–64 and won again in 1970, in spite of the majority of the electorate coming from the working class. This 'cross-class' voting was the result of three factors, as shown in Figure 3.2.

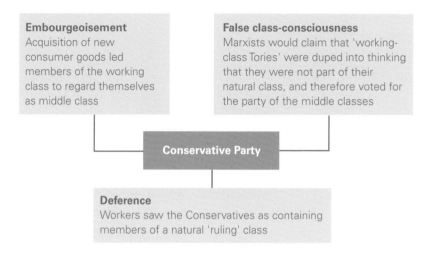

Figure 3.2 Explanations of cross-class voting

- The definition of class is imprecise. Where does one place the company secretary or housewife, for example? The attribution of class is important because not everyone would agree that they are a member of the class attributed to them. Any analysis of their voting habits is likely to be flawed as a result.
- The profound impact of deindustrialisation during the 1980s threw class-based analysis into turmoil as cleavages developed within the working class. As well as the stereotypical unionised manual worker, there was a proliferation of non-unionised clerical workers in the burgeoning service sector. Some commentators argue that it then became impossible to talk about a common class interest among the working class.
- The sharp political decline of the Labour Party after 1979 led some academics to argue that a process of **class dealignment** had taken place, with Labour's natural supporters defecting to different political parties.

Class dealignment

By the mid-1970s, the stable electoral landscape began to take on a very different form: first, support for the two main parties began to ebb away; second, the **volatility** of the electorate increased. That is to say, voters no longer felt as attached, or aligned, to a single party. The idea that a process of dealignment was taking place was first articulated by Ivor Crewe in 1977. The extent of this process is illustrated in Figure 3.3 (absolute class voting is a measure of how many voters actually vote for their 'natural' party).

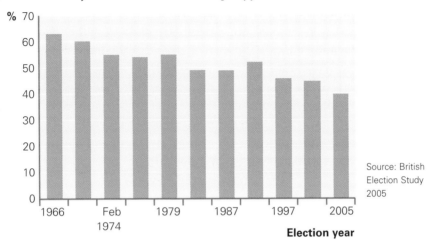

Source: British Election Study 2005

Election year

Figure 3.3 The decline in absolute class voting, 1966–2005

One important effect of dealignment on the political parties is that more voters are inclined to look beyond the two main parties and to cast their vote for an increasingly diverse range of parties. While the extent of Liberal Democrat support has increased since 1979, so too has support for independent, local and marginal parties. One only has to consider the success of Martin Bell at Tatton in 1997, Dr Richard Taylor in Wyre Forest and George Galloway's Respect Party to find evidence of this phenomenon.

George Galloway

The second significant impact of dealignment has been to increase the volatility of the electorate, creating a group of voters whose political preferences cannot be banked on by any of the parties and who are thus more susceptible to the shorter-term influences of the election campaign. It is not surprising that these 'floating' voters are the targets of the most intensive campaigning during the weeks leading up to the election. The size of this group of voters has increased significantly during the era of dealignment. Bob Worcester of the polling organisation MORI estimated that there might have been up to 1 million floating voters in the 2005 election. The factors that swayed the attitudes of these voters

in 2005 are dealt with later in this chapter, but two examples from the campaign illustrate how concerned each party was by the likely impact of large numbers of floating voters in marginal constituencies.

First, the Labour Party developed a project called 'The Big Conversation' in advance of the general election, designed to demonstrate the party's willingness to engage with popular opinion. Fearing a backlash from the effects of the Iraq War and the unpopularity of university tuition fees, the project was, to all intents and purposes, a gigantic public relations exercise, whose roots could be found in the government's obsession with focus groups and the influence of US political consultants and pollsters close to the Labour campaign.

Second, on a more local level, the experience of voters in Cheadle, then the UK's most marginal constituency, is instructive. Throughout the campaign voters were subjected to a daily barrage of leaflets from supporters of the sitting MP, Patsy Calton, a Liberal Democrat, and the previous incumbent, Stephen Day, a Conservative. While this is not uncommon in hotly contested seats, the fact that both parties were prepared to deliver at least two leaflets per day to households, and the overwhelming negativity of both campaigns, illustrate the high premium attached to wavering voters in such a marginal seat.

Learning point

How convincing is the dealignment thesis?

In a direct challenge to the dealignment orthodoxy, Heath, Curtice and Jowell opened a fierce debate on the political loyalties of the UK's social classes. According to their studies of the 1983 and 1987 elections, the extent of dealignment had been exaggerated due to a flawed method of allocating people to classes. In particular, they challenged the usefulness of the manual/non-manual division.

(a) On what grounds do you think the manual/non-manual division can be contested?

(b) How do you think this would lead one to challenge the accuracy of dealignment theory?

Causes of class dealignment

Class dealignment can be explained by a number of factors.

Changes in the structure of the economy

The long-standing period of deindustrialisation and its gradual replacement by a service-dominated economy has had profound social implications. One immediate consequence has been a reduction in the number of manual workers, due partly to the decline of the manufacturing sector, but also to the greater accessibility of higher education.

Education

Increasing voter awareness of differences between parties, and less reliance on emotive attachment to one party, has been facilitated by more people staying on beyond the minimum school-leaving age and subsequently going on to university.

Sectoral cleavages

Another school of thought explains class dealignment by examining structural cleavages within the working class, in particular whether or not workers rely on the public sector for the majority of their services. These might typically include housing, employment, benefits and transport. While these voters would be more likely to vote Labour, members of the working class who were able to 'consume' the majority of their services from the private sector would be more inclined to vote for the Conservatives. This analysis can be broadened to take into account other cleavages, such as union/non-union employment and north/south residence.

Task 3.1

Study Table 3.2. Using the data and your own knowledge, discuss the view that social class is no longer an important determinant in influencing voting behaviour.

Table 3.2 Breakdown of the 2005 general election results by social class (change from 2001 in brackets)

Party	AB (%)	C1 (%)	C2 (%)	DE (%)
Labour	28 (–2)	32 (–6)	40 (–9)	48 (–7)
Conservative	37 (–2)	36 (—)	33 (+4)	25 (+1)
Liberal Democrat	29 (+4)	23 (+3)	19 (+4)	18 (+5)
Others	6	9	8	9

Guidance

There is plenty of evidence in Table 3.2 to support this view. Labour's share of the vote from its natural supporters (C2s and DEs) looks to be in serious decline whereas the Conservatives appear to be gaining votes from C2s and DEs, with their share of the top social group falling. Meanwhile, the Liberal Democrats gained from each of the social groups.

This can be explained by several factors: changing work patterns; education; influence of the media; party strategy.

Task 3.1 (continued)

However, the general direction of each group's voting suggests that class is still an important influence on how people vote. Labour enjoys an overwhelming majority of the vote among the bottom two social groups, and the Conservatives remain the party of choice among AB and C1s.

While it is not the same determining factor that it was during the 'era of alignment', class is still a significant influence on voting behaviour, with almost 40% of votes going with class.

Gender

Until 1997, the accepted wisdom was that women were, politically at least, far more conservative than men. Indeed, a semi-serious piece in the *Sunday Times* once posed the question, 'What would Britain be like if only women had had the vote since the mid-1960s?' The conclusion was that there would have been a succession of Conservative governments, whose character would have differed considerably from those which were actually formed in 1970–74 and 1979–97 (see the Learning Point below for an explanation as to why this would have been the case). The data support this view, as 41% of women, from across the social spectrum, voted Conservative in 1964, compared to only 35% of men.

Learning point

How do women's attitudes differ from men's?

In general:
- Their priorities are focused on equal pay and access to childcare.
- They prefer increased spending on schools and hospitals over tax cuts.
- They favour social welfare elements of the EU.
- They strongly support the return of capital punishment.
- They oppose easier, 'no fault' divorces.

(a) How can you explain the differences in attitudes between women and men?

(b) What evidence is there that Labour has attempted to address women's attitudes more closely since Tony Blair became leader in 1994?

Several reasons have been put forward to explain the psephological phenomenon of gender voting. First, in the past, women were not exposed to the same political and social forces as men. They were less likely to find themselves in unionised employment, for example, partly due to their being more likely to stay at home raising a family. Second, some commentators argue that women are more socially aspirational than men, thus explaining their inclination to vote for a party that seems willing to fulfil these aspirations.

However, following a pattern that has emerged in the USA since 1992, the direction of the female vote has changed: in each election since 1997, the Labour Party has benefited from the women's vote. Indeed, as Table 3.3 suggests, there has been a dramatic role reversal in the importance of men and women to the election of a Labour government.

Table 3.3 Gender and voting in 2005

	Men (%)	Women (%)
Labour	34	38
Conservatives	34	32
Liberal Democrats	23	22

Source: a MORI poll of 18,000 interviewees, May 2005.

If Tony Blair had been able to remove the franchise from men before the election, he might well have found himself with a much more comfortable majority than he actually gained.

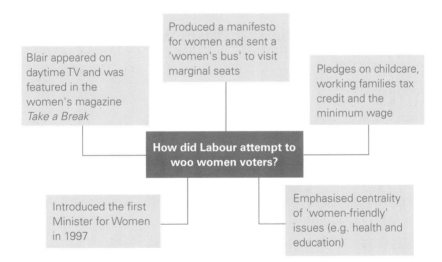

Figure 3.4 New Labour and women voters

However, the importance of the female vote can be qualified if one looks more closely at the behaviour of women across the generations. As the next section explains in greater detail, older voters are more likely to vote Conservative than their younger counterparts. This was certainly true among women in the 2005 election, where 41% of women over the age of 55 voted Conservative, compared to 34% who voted for the Labour Party. What this might suggest, therefore, is that age is a more influential determinant of voting behaviour than gender.

Age

'Young people can afford to be radical', 'socialism is something that you'll grow out of' and other such clichés have passed into popular folklore. But, given that there is an element of truth in most clichés, perhaps there is something in the view that the young tend to cast their vote for more left-wing groups and then move further to the right as they get older. Certainly, evidence from the 2005 election would bear this out. Among all voters aged 18–54, Labour enjoyed a clear majority over each of the other parties, while a lot more people aged 55+ voted for the Conservative Party than for Labour.

Even so, these figures fail to mention some interesting developments in the two youngest age brackets. In one such development, constituencies with large student populations saw Labour's share of the vote fall significantly (see Table 3.4). This might suggest that, in some quarters at least, the Liberal Democrats rather than Labour might now be seen as the natural home for radicals.

| Table 3.4 | Students and the Labour vote in 2005 | | |

Constituency	% of students	% fall in Labour's share of the vote since 2001	Result
Cambridge	25.4	11.1	Liberal Democrat gain from Labour
Liverpool Riverside	22.5	13.8	Labour hold

Source: 'General Election 2005', Parliamentary Research Paper 05/33.

While it might be possible to dismiss the results in Table 3.4 as being unrepresentative of the 18–24 age group as a whole (I have made an assumption about the ages of most of the students in these constituencies), Labour's share of the entire 25–34 vote fell by 13% between 2001 and 2005. Once again, the Liberal Democrats were the principal beneficiaries, increasing their share of the vote among this group by 8% during the same time period.

Why are young people more likely to vote Labour than Conservative?

No definite answer exists to this question, although there are several likely explanations. One theory focuses on the age during which people became politically aware, or active for the first time. According to this view, someone growing up in the Thatcher era could have been radicalised by images of the miners' strike or the poll-tax riots. Similarly, the issue of tuition fees could prove beneficial to the Liberal Democrats in the long term, as a generation of students feels the effect of 'top-up fees' and associates the Liberal Democrats with opposition to this method of financing the expansion of higher education.

Another explanation is less easy to evaluate, having at its heart a belief in youthful idealism. This theory presupposes that young people, free of the family and financial commitments acquired later in life, are more willing to advocate and support radical policies.

One final thought on age: as only 35% of 18–24-year-olds turned out to vote in 2005, compared to 75% of the 55+ group, and with a steadily ageing electorate, perhaps the key to future electoral success lies not in interviews in *Prima* and *Bella*, but in tours of cruise ships and features in *Saga* magazine!

Students protesting against university top-up fees

Region

During the 1980s, where voters lived was presented as a serious contender as the dominant social influence on voting. Indeed, the migration of workers from urban to rural communities, and from north to south, threatened to keep Labour in opposition almost permanently. However, this interpretation was challenged by those who felt that regional factors only really represented existing divisions between classes — for example voters in Wales tended to support the Labour Party because the country contained several large-scale industries, rather than because they lived in Wales.

The 2005 general election offered evidence to support both points of view, as Box 3.1 shows. It can be argued that where you live clearly makes a difference to the type of MP that you will have, but that this is likely to be a result of the inbuilt pro-Labour bias of the electoral system or the social make-up of the constituency.

Box 3.1

How significant were regional factors in the 2005 general election?

Regional factors were significant
- The electoral system was biased against English Conservatives. In England the Conservatives polled 57,000 more votes than Labour, but won 93 fewer seats.
- However, the Conservatives achieved a disproportionately high increase in their number of seats in London and the South East.
- The Conservatives won only four out of 99 seats in Scotland and Wales.

> Box 3.1 (continued)
>
> - Types of constituency proved to be critical in explaining differences with 2001. Labour failed to win as many 'high-status' or 'white-collar' constituencies, while the Conservatives underperformed in 'manufacturing' seats.
> - Irrespective of constituency type, the Conservatives still found it impossible to achieve a major breakthrough north of the Midlands.
>
> **Regional factors were not especially significant**
> - Regional swings tended to be consistent up and down the country. Labour's share of the vote fell by around 6% in all regions.
> - The composition of individual constituencies appears to have been more significant than their location. For example, Labour struggled where there were sizeable Muslim or student communities.
> - The regional element in Liberal Democrat electoral success was reduced, as the party increased its representation in all regions apart from the South East and the Midlands.

Party identification and voting behaviour

A more refined version of the class model of voting was offered by academics from Michigan State University in the 1960s. For this reason, the **partisan (or party) identification** model is often referred to as the 'Michigan model'. Like the class model, it emphasises the importance of 'irrational' influences on a voter's actions. It argues that voters base their choice on a long-term commitment to a party, and pay comparatively little attention to the policy differences between the parties at election time or the performance of the parties since the last election. In this way, voters' loyalty to a party could be compared to their attachment to a particular brand of soap powder, or even to a football team. One could argue that, if true, this simplifies the process of voting, as the voter who identifies so strongly with a party has no real decision to make when casting his or her vote. Barring some sort of political earthquake, voters simply vote as they have always done.

Where the partisan identification model differs from the class model is in arguing that a voter is socialised into adopting a strong identification with a party through important influences in his or her life. These could be family members, friends, teachers, workmates or even religious leaders. Indeed, Butler and Stokes stressed the importance of family members in determining one's political allegiance, but they placed greater emphasis on the *reinforcing* role of socialisation rather than viewing it as a *sole* determinant of voting behaviour.

What is the extent and importance of party identification in the UK?

Until the mid-1970s, it was possible to argue two things about party identification: first, the vast majority of the country 'identified' with a political party and, second, nearly all of them identified with either the Labour or Conservative Party. This meant that very few uncommitted or 'floating' voters existed.

One result of this was a high degree of political stability during the postwar era. Even though the proportion of the voters who regarded themselves as 'strong' identifiers with a party was only around 40%, relatively few voters actually switched sides. Any change of government could therefore be explained by a party losing more of its supporters to its rival, or failing to win over sufficient neutrals during the campaign.

Most studies accept that the majority of the electorate still identifies with one of the major parties. However, there are three significant differences in the way people relate to the Labour and Conservative parties — differences that go some way to explaining the sequence of unusual election results in the UK since 1992:

- *Fewer* people claim to identify with one of the two major parties. At the 2005 general election, 76% of the electorate claimed to do so. This compares unfavourably with the figure from 1964.
- The *extent* of identification has weakened quite dramatically since the 1960s, when around 40% of those eligible to vote were happy to be categorised as having a very strong identification with Labour or Conservative. In 2005, less than 15% of the electorate claimed to identify strongly with a party. Even among those who admitted to identifying with either party, the extent of identification was not particularly strong: only 14% among Conservative supporters and 16% for Labour supporters.
- Bucking the trend of the 1970s and 1980s, in recent years the Conservatives appear to have suffered a greater haemorrhaging of 'identifiers' than Labour.

In spite of this, the weakening of identification has not had a decisive impact on the two-party system of government, as no other party has come close to challenging the ability of the 'big two' to win power.

However, it has led to a notable increase in parliamentary representation for the Liberal Democrats, and for 'independent' candidates such as Martin Bell, Dr Richard Taylor and George Galloway. To put this into context, Peter Kellner of the opinion pollsters YouGov has argued that, although approximately

44% of the electorate identified with Labour at the last election, the lack of strong identifiers meant that a sizeable chunk of that 44% chose to vote for another party.

What factors have contributed to weakening partisanship?

The weakening of party identification in the UK has been caused by several factors.

Performance of the parties and their leaders

Underpinning a voter's partisanship is a belief that their preferred party will ultimately implement policies that will benefit them. It goes without saying that this attachment will be eroded if they lose faith in the ability of their party to effectively represent their interests.

In 1955, almost half the electorate approved of the Conservative government's record in office, and around 55% believed that the prime minister had done a good job. During the last 50 years, however, public perception of government and opposition performance has become somewhat more critical, largely as a result of successive governments of different ideological persuasions being unable to fulfil the promises they made in election manifestos.

The most extreme example of a government being on the receiving end of public disdain was between 1992 and 1997, when John Major's government recorded approval levels of just 15% at its point of lowest popularity. The Conservatives failed to make a better impression when in opposition after 1997, and even the Blair government, with three successive election victories, cannot claim to enjoy huge amounts of public confidence. The 2001 victory was achieved with a record low turnout, and in 2005 the party retained power with only 35% of the popular vote.

Ideological disjuncture

During the golden era of partisanship, both main parties remained true to a broadly consistent ideological package. One explanation for weakening partisanship is that both parties moved away from their core support, and as a consequence undermined the attachment felt by its partisan supporters. For Labour, this process occurred during the early 1980s, when the party lurched to the left under the leadership of Michael Foot. The Conservative Party, too, was guilty of moving away from its traditional voter base by the end of its 18-year period in office. This was, in part, because of public unrest at the less palatable effects of the government's privatisation programme, and a feeling that institutions such as the NHS were being undermined by creeping privatisation.

The impact of the media

While it is very difficult to draw a direct line between increasing media attention to political life and weakening partisanship, it does not require a huge leap of faith to accept that the more we learn about parties and politicians, the more likely we are to question long-held preconceptions and attitudes. This is especially true when one takes into account the increasingly critical approach of the media to politicians of all sides, and the cynicism towards public figures that this engenders. Whether it is a former deputy leader of the Labour Party being symbolised by a tub of lard on *Have I Got News For You*, or the leaders of all the major parties submitting to a trial by ordeal by a group of voters on *Question Time* during the 2005 campaign, politicians can no longer rely on the media to present an uncritical impression.

A subtle change in the way political news is reported has also contributed to this process. Coverage of the 2005 campaign suggested that television news editors no longer trusted the electorate to make up their own minds about events and policy statements; it has been suggested that more time was spent providing 'on the spot' analysis than on descriptions of the day's events.

For the media to have any impact at all on popular opinion, people have, first, to be exposed to the message and, second, to believe in it. Evidence from the 2005 campaign highlights a long-standing problem with television coverage of politics in the UK, namely that the number of viewers tuning in to watch political programmes or politics-dominated news is declining. Between 1992 and 2005, the audience for the BBC main news bulletins fell by 34%. The decline in viewers for ITV during the same period was even greater.

To what extent do voters act 'rationally'?

In the 1950s, electoral studies were revolutionised by the work of Anthony Downs. He did not agree with the view that voters based their electoral preferences on long-term sociological factors, or indeed that a high level of party identification still existed. Instead, he argued that voters treated political parties in the same way that they treated consumer goods, and therefore based their choice at election time on the likely 'costs' and 'benefits' of voting for a particular party.

Although some, undecided, voters might have paid attention to campaigns and policy positions during the era of alignment, the impact of issues was only felt to be short term and partial. However, as the electoral landscape changed, and evidence emerged about the decline of class and partisan alignment, **rational voting** appeared to offer a more credible explanation for electoral behaviour.

Rational voting is, in itself, a large area of study, and not all subscribers to the theory accept the relevance of all aspects. The main subdivisions of rational voting are:

- issue voting
- the economy
- the impact of the party leaders

Issue voting

There are two principal issue-voting models: the **spatial model** and the **valence model**.

The spatial model

In his original study, Downs argued that parties that avoided extreme positions on the majority of issues would appeal to the highest number of voters. His conclusion, therefore, was that a successful party had to position itself in the middle ground of a left–right political spectrum, in order to avoid alienating large numbers of possible supporters. This would appear to have been borne out by the failure of the Labour Party to win power in the 1980s with an agenda that was regarded as too 'socialist' by the electorate, and by the Conservatives' failure since 1997. The Conservative Party was seen as moving too far to the right in an attempt to distinguish itself from a centrist Labour Party. While it succeeded in stabilising its core vote in 2001 and 2005, it still failed to broaden its appeal beyond its natural supporters.

This spatial model of voting (so called because parties have to occupy the median space on a left–right political spectrum) has been criticised for offering an outdated and overly simplistic analysis. It is argued that:

- The traditional political spectrum is no longer relevant to UK politics. Voters are capable of holding positions that are ideologically inconsistent. Positioning yourself at 'the centre', therefore, would not automatically guarantee political success.
- As the differences between the main parties have lessened, so too has the relevance of the spatial model. If policies on law and order and the economy are virtually indistinguishable, how can voters judge the parties on their approach to them?
- The spatial model assumes that voters base their choices on **prospective** judgements, that is, on who will be most likely to act in a way that is consistent with their convictions. Recent research suggests that **retrospective** judgements form popular opinion better. A retrospective judgement is based on what a party or government has already done, and not on what it promises to do when in office.

Learning point

How do people vote rationally?

In what ways do the small viewing figures for television election coverage and the poor sales of party manifestos undermine the issue-voting model?

The valence model

A competing model of issue voting is the valence model. It argues that voters place emphasis on the ability of parties to deliver effective policies on issues that are more general and virtually uncontested. Examples of valence issues might be 'prosperity', 'safer streets' and 'successful schools'.

The valence model contains a sub-model that concerns the **salience**, or relevance, of an issue at the time. Parties clearly believe that this is an important influence on voting behaviour, because they spend much of the campaign attempting to impose their issue agenda on the election and in the process persuade the voters what the most salient issues of the day are. Rival valence agendas in 2005 are shown in Box 3.2.

> Box 3.2
> **Rival valence agendas in the 2005 campaign**
>
> | Labour | Conservative |
> |---|---|
> | Economic success | Asylum seekers |
> | Public service delivery | Security |

How important was issue voting in 2005?

The British Election Study surveyed a range of people during the 2005 campaign. Figure 3.5 adapts its findings on the issues that voters regarded as most important, and which main party was seen as the most competent on each of these issues.

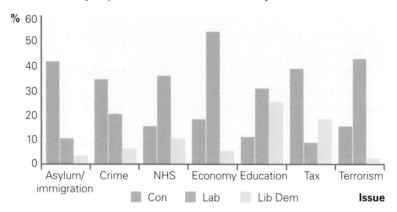

Figure 3.5 Voters' views of which main party was most competent on the principal election issues, 2005

Several observations can be made about the importance of issue voting in 2005:

- Valence issues dominated the campaign. Spatial, or position, issues such as civil liberties feature a long way down the list of priorities. Surprisingly, only 2% of respondents believed the Iraq War was the most important issue.
- Spatial issues did play a part in boosting Liberal Democrat representation, however, with a large majority of voters stating that the Liberal Democrats had the best approach to the environment, civil liberties and Iraq.
- Labour enjoyed a clear lead over the Conservatives on the majority of the most important issues. However, when all responses and issues were factored in, no one party enjoyed a significant lead in the issue agenda.
- Issues that the electorate regards as important do not always remain constant between elections. Asylum, crime and terrorism — issues that did not feature prominently in 2001 — were mentioned by 41% of respondents in 2005.
- Opinion about the most competent party overall changes over time as well. In 2001, 39% believed Labour was likely to be the most competent, with only 14% support for the Conservatives. In 2005, the Conservative score rose to 26% and Labour's fell to 23%.

With only 23% of the electorate believing that the Labour Party was the strongest on the issues, issue voting by itself cannot provide a satisfactory explanation of Labour's victory. This leads us to consider more general criticisms of issue voting as a whole.

- The link between issues and votes can be regarded as tenuous. Some analysts have cast doubt on the public's awareness of what each party's position on an issue is. During the 1980s, polls suggested that unemployment and the NHS were the most important issues, yet the electorate voted for Conservative governments in 1983 and 1987 with large parliamentary majorities.
- Both forms of issue voting ignore the manipulative effect of the media. Most newspapers were aligned with one of the parties during the 2005 campaign, and even television news can influence people's attitudes merely by ranking stories in a particular order of importance.
- The prioritisation of issues by opinion poll respondents may simply reflect the priorities of their preferred party.
- Similarly, when the valence model is analysed, perceptions of competence might also reflect general partisanship.
- Voters do not always make their decisions purely on isolated issues. Instead, they consider more general values and beliefs of political parties to be important. For example, they might take into account a party's attitudes towards the role of the state, or citizens' rights and liberties etc.

The economy

Arguably the strongest card in Labour's possession in 2005 was its impressive economic record since coming to power. It is one of the givens of politics that the state of the economy is the most important issue in people's minds as they approach the ballot box. There are two main ways of exploring the impact of economic performance on the electorate: one that focuses on perception of economic prosperity, and the other that examines the link between electoral cycles and the economy (see Box 3.3).

Box 3.3

Two models of economic performance and voting behaviour

Economic perceptions
- Early analysis presupposed that the party in power generally wins elections during periods of prosperity.
- The 1992 Conservative victory (during a recession) and the 1997 Conservative defeat (during a boom) challenged this analysis.
- A more sophisticated view relies on either retrospective/prospective judgements or an assessment of individual or collective economic well-being.
- The evidence from the 2005 British Election Survey data is consistent with the election result. Less than a quarter of the respondents believed the situation would improve in the next year, but a sizeable minority thought things would stay the same.

Electoral cycles and the economy
- This model relies on regular poll findings about the state of the economy.
- It is sometimes referred to as a study of the 'feel-good factor'.
- By aggregating the responses, it is possible to predict the popularity of the government accurately.
- The biggest influences on attitudes towards the economy are the level of the interest rate and the rate of inflation.

Both attempts to evaluate the links between economic performance and electoral behaviour have been subject to critical appraisal.

One of the biggest problems with this theory of voting, in common with other forms of issue voting, is the difficulty of detaching existing political attitudes from perceptions of the economy. It would not be too surprising to find opponents of the government viewing the performance of the economy in less positive terms than its supporters.

Even so, very few commentators would deny that the performance of the economy has a significant bearing on how people make their choices at election time.

The impact of the party leaders

During the era of class and partisan alignment, the impact of the party leader was regarded as insignificant. The reason for this is that long-term forces of social class and environmental socialisation would have overridden the temporary consideration of who was in charge of a party. Essentially, the factors that led the voter to identify with a party would remain constant, irrespective of who the leader was.

However, supporters of dealignment theory argue that the importance of the party leadership has increased significantly, to the extent that, as one commentator argued, public dissatisfaction with Tony Blair could have cost the party up to 12 percentage points in 2005.

This section outlines how the importance of leaders has increased since the mid-1970s, and then examines the impact of each party leader during the 2005 election.

Figure 3.6 demonstrates the relative importance of a party's choice of leader since 1983. In each election, a strong case can be made that the impact of the leadership either swung the result of the election (1992) or made a difference to the size of the majority (1983, 1987, 1997, 2005).

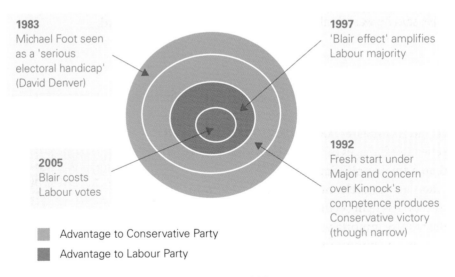

1983
Michael Foot seen as a 'serious electoral handicap' (David Denver)

1997
'Blair effect' amplifies Labour majority

2005
Blair costs Labour votes

1992
Fresh start under Major and concern over Kinnock's competence produces Conservative victory (though narrow)

Advantage to Conservative Party

Advantage to Labour Party

Figure 3.6 Impact of party leaders since 1983

What difference did the party leaders make in 2005?

- **Tony Blair** remained the most popular choice of prime minister in successive YouGov polls. He was a strong factor for people voting Labour, but equally a significant deterrent to those who rated other leaders more highly and who eventually voted for other parties. Evans and Andersen in 'The impact of Party Leaders: how Blair cost Labour votes' in *Britain Votes 2005* (edited by P. Norris and C. Wlezien) claim that a small increase in Blair's popularity would have gained Labour over 40% of the vote.

- **Michael Howard** was rated highly by Conservative voters, suggesting that the party was right to install him in place of Iain Duncan Smith in 2003. He improved on the popularity of his predecessor, but failed to convince the wider electorate that he was prime-ministerial material.
- **Charles Kennedy** regularly topped polls for the most capable party leader. However, although he enjoyed positive approval ratings, the fact that relatively few people voted for his party suggests that other, longer-term factors had more influence on people's attitudes towards the Liberal Democrats.

As well as having a bearing on the direction of public support across the board, the image of each leader proved to be a critical factor in the minds of voters in marginal constituencies. A series of MORI polls found that only 32% of such voters trusted Blair to tell the truth and, by the time of the election, Howard enjoyed a small lead on this issue. That this did not prove to be the ultimate undoing of the government was probably due to the fact that a majority of marginal constituents think Blair has more positive all-round qualities than his opposition counterparts: 44% said he was likeable, compared to only 32% for Howard.

How important is perception of the party leader relative to other influences on voting behaviour?

As with other areas of rational voting, it is difficult to isolate one single factor from existing partisan attitudes. Similarly, voters may be more influenced by generalised images of the parties and its leaders rather than a single politician.

Recent research by the British Election Study throws new light on the issue, however. By comparing the relative importance of factors, it deduced that the two most important determinants of electoral behaviour in 2005 were **partisan identification** and the leadership of the parties. This proved to be the case for supporters of all three main parties and in comparison with social and 'rational' factors.

This would reinforce the beliefs of the parties themselves, which have contributed to a growing 'Americanisation' of election campaigns. This has been evident on many levels. The biographical party

Charles Kennedy as Liberal Democrat leader

political broadcasts (1987's 'Kinnock: the Movie', and 1997's 'Tony's Kitchen' being two of the most notorious) are the most visible example of this trend, but greater use of leaders' wives and new-born babies (Kennedy) in the media, and the relegation of other senior party members to peripheral roles, including the chancellor of exchequer in the earliest stages of the 2005 campaign, are all commonplace in the modern political age.

Task 3.2

If the popularity of Tony Blair and Michael Howard had remained constant during the 2005 general election campaign, but if Charles Kennedy's had increased, it is estimated that his party would have remained on around 23% of the vote.

What might this tell us about the importance of the Kennedy leadership to his party until the end of 2005, and the potential for growth in Liberal Democrat support in future?

Guidance

It suggests that the popularity of the party leader only matters to the two biggest parties. Indeed, like his predecessor (Paddy Ashdown), Charles Kennedy consistently enjoyed positive approval ratings, usually higher than the poll ratings achieved by his party, yet he only managed to achieve marginal political gains.

As far as the potential for Liberal Democrat support is concerned, it could mean one of two things. Either the party should focus less on presenting its leader as a rival to the leaders of the Conservative and Labour parties, and instead work harder at building the profile of the party and its ideas; or it could suggest that the party has effectively reached a plateau of support. If the party leader does have an overall impact on a party's level of support — and Kennedy *was* seen as an asset — then it is unlikely that the Liberal Democrats will be able to improve on their current levels of support under the existing electoral system.

To what extent does tactical voting affect the results of general elections?

What is 'tactical voting'?

Tactical or 'insincere' **voting** takes place when a supporter of a party with little chance of winning a constituency transfers his or her vote to another party in an attempt to prevent the leading party from winning the seat again. A good example of this in action is provided in Table 3.5, which gives the results for the constituency of Leeds North West in 2001 and 2005 and demonstrates the impact of some Conservatives switching tactically to the Liberal Democrats.

Table 3.5 General election result for Leeds North West, 2005 (2001 figures in brackets)

Candidate	Share of the vote (%)	
G. Mulholland (Lib Dem)	37.15	(26.93)
J. Blake (Lab)	32.96	(41.92)
G. Lee (Con)	25.74	(29.58)
M. Hemingway (Green)	2.52	

Tactical voting has grown in popularity and significance since the early 1990s, when it became clear that the swing to Labour was greatest in Conservative/Labour marginals.

Influences on the decision to vote tactically can be diverse. Usually, one assumes that a willing tactical voter is aware of the national situation and of the impact that a favourable result in his or her constituency will have on the final outcome of the election.

Voters' decisions could also be swung by media reports. In April 1997, the *Observer* newspaper declared on the Sunday before the election that recent polls in the constituency of Enfield Southgate placed the Labour challenger only 5 points behind the sitting MP, Michael Portillo, a symbol at the time of all that was deemed unpalatable in the Conservative government. Its message was clear: with the support of Liberal Democrat voters, Portillo could be unseated the following Thursday. The newspaper's campaign paid off, as Labour candidate Stephen Twigg was elected on a swing of 17% from Portillo.

How has the operation of tactical voting developed in recent years?

The working of tactical voting has changed in several ways:
- The Conservatives are no longer the prime target of tactical voters; instead, the new victim appears to be the Labour Party. However, there are exceptions to this rule, as the election results for Cheadle, in the North West, show (see Task 3.3).
- It could be argued that the purpose of tactical voting has subtly changed. In 2005, the electorate seemed capable of using this procedure to deliver a 'bloody nose' to Tony Blair's government, that is, keeping him in power, but with a much reduced majority. The Labour vote fell most sharply in its own seats, with the Liberal Democrats appearing to be the prime beneficiaries where they had previously lain second to Labour.

• Voters have demonstrated a greater willingness to organise tactical voting on a mass scale and across different constituencies.

It appears that tactical voting remains an important factor in deciding not just who holds power, but critically how much power they have to exercise. However, the chance of Liberal Democrat and Conservative voters helping each other out in order to unseat Labour at the next election still seems quite remote, given the substantial ideological gap between the parties.

Task 3.3

Study Table 3.6 carefully and answer the questions that follow.

Table 3.6 Election results for Cheadle, 2001–05

Party	Share of the vote (%)
2001 general election	
P. Calton (Lib Dem)	42.37
S. Day (Con)	42.30
H. Dawber (Lab)	13.96
2005 general election	
P. Calton (Lib Dem)	48.88
S. Day (Con)	40.41
M. Miller (Lab)	8.79
2005 by-election	
M. Hunter (Lib Dem)	52.15
S. Day (Con)	42.30
M. Miller (Lab)	4.63

(a) What evidence is there for the existence of tactical voting during each of the 2005 elections in Cheadle?

(b) What are the main arguments against the use of tactical voting?

Guidance

(a) Look carefully at the vote share for the Liberal Democrat and Labour candidates. The Liberal Democrat majority in 2001 was 33 votes, so non-Conservatives knew that the Conservative candidate would have a good chance of retaking the seat in 2005. As a result, the already small Labour vote falls by 5%, which, along with a small defection of disillusioned Conservatives, is sufficient to keep the Conservatives out. The pattern is repeated, but to a much greater extent in the by-election that followed the death of the Liberal Democrat MP. The Labour vote falls once again, down 9% on its 2001 score, and the Liberal Democrat increases

Task 3.3 (continued)

still further. Meanwhile, the Conservative vote has fluctuated very little, moving no more than 2% throughout the period of the three elections.

(b) The arguments against tactical voting include:

- It contravenes the positive elements of representative democracy, as it is more concerned with preventing somebody from being elected than with selecting the best candidate to represent the interests of constituents.
- It also serves to restrict voter choice in the long term, as the position of the two most popular parties becomes entrenched and the third party gradually removes resources from the constituency. Thus, supporters of a major party are effectively denied the opportunity to vote for it.
- The biggest influence on voters is likely to be the result of the previous election, so changing political and economic circumstances in the intervening period are irrelevant.
- It is usually targeted at one party. Between 1997 and 2001, the Conservatives suffered badly at the hands of tactical voters, but much of the evidence from 2005 indicates that Labour has now become the main victim.
- It can encourage unfair electoral practice. During the 2005 general election, the Liberal Democrats in Cheadle were criticised for producing elections leaflets in red ink, designed to look as if they were produced by the Labour Party. This was supposedly done to make Labour voters think that their party advocated voting for the Liberal Democrats in Cheadle.

Conclusion: why do we vote the way we do?

For all the theories, data analysis and new interpretations, the last 30 years have seen relative consistency in the factors that most influence how we vote. Given the post-industrial splintering of the working class, it has become increasingly difficult to discuss the leaning of that particular class in any meaningful sense. When one also considers the deliberate repositioning of that social group's 'natural' party, it could be seen as quaintly old-fashioned to link Labour closely with any form of manual or low-paid work.

For all the interest they generate, other social factors lack the distinctive influence to be regarded as significant. While the rise of New Labour has coincided with the changing direction of the female vote, this has largely been offset by the ageing nature of the UK's population — a development that most benefits the Conservative Party.

Does this mean that we are all cold, analytical, rational voters then? Here, too, there are problems. It is difficult to equate an electorate that shows decreasing interest in all forms of political communication, coupled with an ambivalent approach to voting, with one that has a firm grasp of issue salience, can distinguish between different policy standpoints and can then vote for the party most closely positioned to their own. Fundamentally, it assumes a level of voter interest and sophistication that the evidence suggests is markedly absent.

What we are left with, therefore, is the continuing importance of partisan identification and the growing personalisation of elections. The 2005 election demonstrates most clearly that the advantage Labour enjoys among partisan voters continues to keep it ahead of its rivals. This identification also informs a wide range of responses given to opinion pollsters on such things as the state of the economy, valence issues and the performance of party leaders. However, significant question marks over the capabilities of Tony Blair as prime minister ultimately proved critical in undermining the lead that his party enjoyed among partisan identifiers.

Useful websites

- Tacticalvoter.net
  www.tacticalvoter.net
- tacticalvoter.org.uk
  www.tactical-voter.org.uk
- YouGov
  www.yougov.com

Further reading

- Denver, D. (2003) *Elections and Voters in Britain*, Palgrave Macmillan.
- Norris, P. and Wlezien, C. (eds) (2005) *Britain Votes 2005*, Oxford University Press in association with the Hansard Society.

Chapter 4

How important is the electoral campaign?

No self-respecting election campaign would be complete without its team of private pollsters, campaign managers, researchers, rebuttal units, hard-bitten US election gurus, distinctly off-message punch-ups, 'spontaneous' meetings between the party leaders and pre-selected members of the public, and embarrassing moments when the prime minister meets a disgruntled 'real' voter. Factor in an estimated cost of £15 million and what you have is one expensive exercise in virtual politics. Four weeks of saturation politics, months of planning, and still only 60% of the electorate are sufficiently moved to go out and vote.

Subscribers to dealignment theory would argue that the campaign plays a much greater role in affecting electoral behaviour now than it did during the earlier aligned era. This is largely due to the absence of socialising influences and the decline in partisanship. This chapter is primarily concerned with the features and significance of election campaigns, and all that they entail. The main theme of the debate is whether they actually make a difference to the way that people vote, or whether they consist of nothing but bluster, camouflaging the fact that the fates of the parties have already been decided in the preceding months and years.

In order to tackle the key issue, it will be necessary to discuss the role of features that either may contribute to the effectiveness of the campaign, such as party funding and the role of the media, or might be seen as *symptoms* of an effective campaign, in this case turnout. Finally, we shall examine the role and accuracy of the device used to measure the impact of the campaign: opinion polls. Specific attention will also be paid to the nature of the 2005 campaign, and how it contributed to the final result on 5 May.

Funding the campaign

How much do parties spend on elections?

The 1997 general election was the most expensive on record. In the year before the election, the three leading parties spent a combined total of £58 million, £28 million of it being spent by the Conservatives. Legislation was introduced

in 2000 that placed a limit on how much parties could spend nationally in the year before polling day.

The Political Parties, Elections and Referendums Act (PPERA) 2000 introduced a ceiling of £30,000 per seat contested. For the parties that contested all 646 seats, that set a limit of £19.38 million. Individual seat limits depend on the number of constituents and the nature of the constituency. In 2001 spending limits ranged from £6,846 in the Western Isles to £11,957 in the Isle of Wight. The Act is also very clear about the different categories of expenditure that may be incurred by parties, and covers areas such as party political broadcasts, advertising, manifestos and transport.

Learning point
Election spending

| Table 4.1 | Levels of election spending in 2005 (£m) (2001 spending in brackets) |

Labour	17.94	(10.94)
Conservatives	17.85	(12.75)
Liberal Democrats	4.32	(1.36)
Total	40.11	(25.05)

Source: the Electoral Commission

(a) Why do you think the Liberal Democrats' level of expenditure is some way below that of the other main parties?

(b) Research the number of votes and seats won by each party. Which party got most value for money for its spending?

Where do parties get the money from?

As a result of several scandals revolving around the issue of 'cash for questions', the Committee on Standards in Public Life (the Neill Committee) recommended the introduction of controls on political donations.

Box 4.1

Cash for influence?

In 1994, Conservative MPs Neil Hamilton, Jonathan Aitken, Graham Riddick, David Tredinnick and Tim Smith were accused of receiving payments and gifts from Mohammed Al-Fayed in return for help in getting him a UK passport. In 1997 it emerged that the Labour Party had accepted a £1 million donation from Formula 1 chief Bernie Ecclestone, at a time when his sport was granted exemption from the ban on tobacco advertising. Labour continued to be dogged by accusations of selling access for cash. Paul Drayson, owner of vaccine company Powderject, provided over £1 million for party funds in 2001–05. In 2002 Powderject was given a £32 million contract by the NHS, and Mr Drayson was made a life peer in 2004.

The PPERA was the result of Lord Neill's recommendations, and laid down the following laws regarding political donations:

- Donations of more than £200 to a party or £50 to an individual can only be received from donors either registered to vote or functioning as a business in the UK.
- Anonymous donations must be returned.
- All donations received by local parties for more than £1,000 must be reported to the Electoral Commission, while the national party has to report donations of more than £5,000.
- Any company that wishes to donate to a political party has to seek approval from its shareholders.

Does the amount of expenditure affect the result?

A small amount of evidence exists that suggests that money can buy you (electoral) love. In its report on the 2001 campaign, the Electoral Commission discovered that in 26 of the 29 seats that changed hands, the victorious candidate spent more than 80% of the permitted total.

One could also make a link between the huge gulf between the 'big two' and Liberal Democrat spending both before and during the campaign, and the similar gulf in the number of seats won in the House of Commons. Having the financial capability to implement a comprehensive nationwide campaign, even months before the official start date, gives you a huge political advantage.

However, it is worth going back to the amount spent by the Conservative Party in 1997, and remembering that this was also the worst election result in the party's history.

Should there be state funding of political parties?

A small amount of money is already provided by the state to fund parliamentary work: it is called Short Money (for the Commons) and Cranborne Money (for the Lords). Parties also receive over £20 million in free election mailshots and enjoy free airtime for party political broadcasts.

Several countries have attempted to remove all possibility of accusations that access is being exchanged for cash, by introducing either partial or complete state funding of political parties. In France, after state assistance was introduced in 1988, corporate donations were banned in 1994 and a limit placed on election expenditure. In Germany and Australia, similar rules exist where the state makes a contribution to parties' expenses, so long as they achieve a certain threshold of votes.

The main debate over state funding of political parties is outlined in Box 4.2.

Box 4.2

State funding of political parties: for and against

Advantages

- At present the Liberal Democrats are at a disadvantage as they do not receive as much from large donors as Labour and the Conservatives. Labour also benefits enormously from its union links.
- State funding removes suspicion of large donors buying influence with a party.
- It prevents parties from experiencing financial difficulties between elections (in July 2004 the Conservatives had to leave and try to sell off their HQ at Smith Square to pay off a £2.5m pre-election loan).
- State funding would enable parties to devote more time to political education and policy research.

Disadvantages

- Unions fear it could lead to the Labour leadership removing union influence from the party permanently.
- Taxpayers might resent their taxes being used to finance parties they oppose.
- Some opponents claim taxes could be better spent improving public services, such as hospitals.
- Any system based on parliamentary representation would make it even more difficult for minority parties to compete with the more established parties.

The only provision of state funding for campaign work in the UK at present is during a referendum. The PPERA stipulated that a grant should be provided to both the 'yes' and 'no' campaigns in any future referendum in the UK. This is to ensure a minimum level of campaigning on both sides.

The impact of the media
Why do the media play such an important role during the campaign?

During the last election, the only way that members of the public could get a first-hand view of Tony Blair was if they were a journalist working for one of the media companies given permission to accompany him on his nationwide campaign (BBC, ITN, Sky, the Press Association), inside a television studio (for example, in the audience for his appearance on *Question Time*), or if they were one of the party workers organised to greet him whenever he arrived in a particular constituency. Even if you were lucky enough to come across a party leader in the street, you would barely have had time to engage him or her in serious debate given their need to visit as many battleground seats as possible.

Tony Blair is interviewed by David Frost for the BBC

The 2005 campaign contrasted markedly even with those of relatively recent elections such as 1992 and 1997, when Prime Minister John Major was prepared to do a bit of old-fashioned political campaigning with his literal take on getting on one's soap box.

Essentially, as access to politicians becomes more difficult, the role of the media in presenting images of the leaders and summaries of their ideas becomes considerably more important.

How far do the media shape voting preferences?

The national press

The front page of the *Sun* newspaper on the morning of the 1992 general election featured a picture of the head of the then Labour leader, Neil Kinnock, inside a light bulb. The accompanying headline read 'IF KINNOCK WINS TODAY, WILL THE LAST PERSON TO LEAVE BRITAIN PLEASE TURN OUT THE LIGHTS'. The following morning's edition, after a narrow Conservative victory, led with the headline 'IT'S THE SUN WOT WON IT'. The Conservative Party chairman in 1992 was so grateful for the media's support during the campaign that he dubbed the editors of the Conservative-supporting *Sun* and *Daily Express* as the real heroes of the election.

The bias of the press was considerably tilted towards the Conservatives up until 1997, when a radical realignment took place. Mirroring the transformation that was taking place on the political landscape, the press shifted its allegiance to the Labour Party, with even the *Sun* advocating a Labour victory. While this pattern remained broadly intact in 2001, the situation in 2005 became more fluid, with some commentators arguing that a process of partisan dealignment had taken place among the national press. Using the theory developed by Deacon, Golding and Billig, it is possible to represent the distribution of media support for the main parties as shown in Figure 4.1.

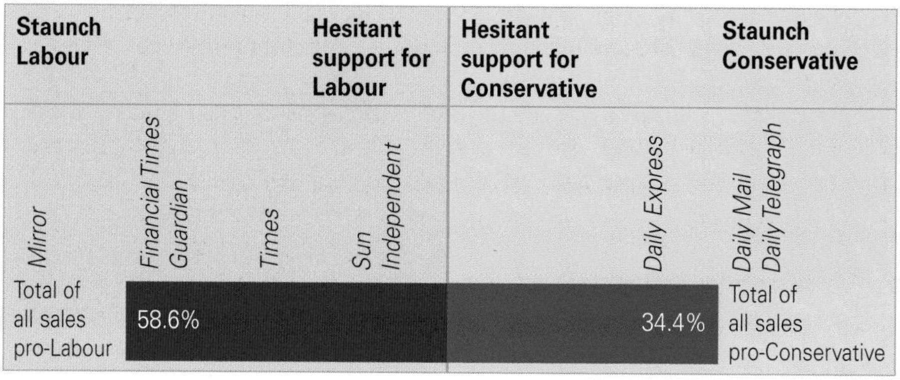

Staunch Labour				Hesitant support for Labour	Hesitant support for Conservative		Staunch Conservative
Mirror	*Financial Times* *Guardian*	*Times*	*Sun* *Independent*		*Daily Express*	*Daily Mail* *Daily Telegraph*	
Total of all sales pro-Labour	58.6%				34.4%	Total of all sales pro-Conservative	

Figure 4.1 Media support for the main parties, 2005

Has this subtle change in the press's endorsement of political parties helped us reach any firm conclusions about the impact of newspapers? Do the printed media really have such an impact on how we vote?

In theory, the answer should be yes, as voters are less partisan and thus more susceptible to a wider range of influences. However, as Box 4.3 suggests, there are significant questions to be asked about the ability of the press to shape voters' preferences during the campaign.

Box 4.3

Do newspapers influence how we vote?

Yes

- A clear link exists between the newspaper that voters read, and the party they eventually vote for. In 2005 66% of *Mirror* readers voted Labour, while 64% of *Daily Telegraph* readers voted for the Conservatives. In general, Labour and Liberal Democrat support was highest among readers of 'sympathetic' papers.
- The impact of dealignment could be argued to have increased the influence of the press, with voters being more likely to follow the lead of their chosen newspaper.
- Long-term research has found that readers who take a pro-Labour or pro-Conservative paper for a considerable period of time are more likely to stay loyal to that party than people who do not read a newspaper.
- Readers of traditionally pro-Conservative papers that changed allegiance in 1997 may have been influenced to change their voting preferences as well.

Box 4.3 (continued)

No

- Most readers buy a paper that already reflects their own political views. The role of the press is therefore only to reinforce the attitudes of voters.
- The shift in the position of many papers in 1997 may have simply resulted from a reluctance to lose readers — they simply reflected the changing attitudes of their readership.
- The extent to which press support can boost a party's standing during the election is also questionable. Labour received the endorsement of the vast majority of papers in 1997, yet its poll ratings actually fell during the campaign. Despite receiving considerable press support in 2005, Labour's poll ratings barely fluctuated at all.
- The number and direction of voters who did switch camps were similar between those groups who did read a newspaper and those who did not.
- One of the major flaws with the argument in favour of media influence is that it cannot explain the variations in levels of support for the Liberal Democrats. Not one daily paper unequivocally endorsed the Liberal Democrats in 2005, yet the party won ten more seats than in 2001, and during the course of the campaign its poll ratings improved, albeit marginally. The *Guardian* came closest to encouraging its readership to vote Lib Dem, but in the end it still plumped for Labour.

In conclusion, it is important to make two points. First, any influence that the press might have wished to exert may have been diminished by the confusing messages several of them put out. The *Sun*, for example, was endorsing Labour but appeared to be more sympathetic towards Conservative policies. The *Independent* argued for a Labour-dominated parliament, but one which comprised more Liberal Democrat MPs.

Second, newspapers do not exist in a vacuum. They know which way public opinion is blowing and, as the experience of both 2001 and 2005 illustrates, refine their stance accordingly. This means not only that their political direction changes, but also that they reflect a growing disillusionment with politics in the UK; research conducted during the campaign found that 75% of tabloid front pages featured non-election stories.

Television

None of the terrestrial broadcasters could be accused of implementing a one-dimensional approach to its coverage of the election. Viewers were presented with an astonishing array of election-related programmes, ranging from the traditional *Question Time* approach to a programme plotting the response of a group of Nottingham students to the election.

However, it has proven notoriously difficult to provide any direct link between television coverage and actual voting behaviour. In the 1960s, studies dismissed the impact of television, arguing that **partisan identification** created a natural filter between the viewer/voter and what was being shown on the television. The end of this era did not bring forth a glut of new studies demonstrating the power of television during campaigns, and even today much greater attention is paid to the influence of the printed press than to that of broadcasters.

In spite of this, one can identify a small number of ways in which the television coverage of the 2005 campaign can be seen as significant (see Figure 4.2).

Learning point

Follow the Sun*?*

- When the *Sun* supported the Conservatives, surveys suggested that most of its readers thought that it was a Labour paper.
- In 2005 it supported Labour, but advocated Conservative policies on the EU and immigration.

Should these two observations influence our impressions about the impact of the media on electoral behaviour?

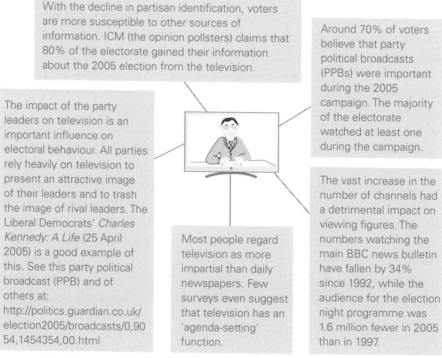

With the decline in partisan identification, voters are more susceptible to other sources of information. ICM (the opinion pollsters) claims that 80% of the electorate gained their information about the 2005 election from the television.

Around 70% of voters believe that party political broadcasts (PPBs) were important during the 2005 campaign. The majority of the electorate watched at least one during the campaign.

The impact of the party leaders on television is an important influence on electoral behaviour. All parties rely heavily on television to present an attractive image of their leaders and to trash the image of rival leaders. The Liberal Democrats' *Charles Kennedy: A Life* (25 April 2005) is a good example of this. See this party political broadcast (PPB) and of others at: http://politics.guardian.co.uk/election2005/broadcasts/0,9054,1454354,00.html

Most people regard television as more impartial than daily newspapers. Few surveys even suggest that television has an 'agenda-setting' function.

The vast increase in the number of channels had a detrimental impact on viewing figures. The numbers watching the main BBC news bulletin have fallen by 34% since 1992, while the audience for the election night programme was 1.6 million fewer in 2005 than in 1997.

Figure 4.2 How does television influence how we vote?

The internet

Following on from its innovative use by supporters of Howard Dean during the 2004 presidential primaries, and the emergence of a 'blogger culture' as a de facto 'Fourth Estate' in the USA, much was expected of the internet in the 2005 UK general election.

Since 2004, political **blogs** have become the attack vehicle of choice for most serious political contenders in the USA. To the unknowing, they appear to be independent providers of opinion, written with no official party allegiance. However, their partisan nature and influence can be illustrated by their role in the defeat of Tom Daschle in 2004, the first Senate party leader to be defeated since 1952. The two leading blogs covering the contest in South Dakota were both written by men on the payroll of the Republican Party. As their blogs contained no reference to this, the impression of political neutrality gave their analysis of Daschle's flaws added credibility.

The 2005 UK election campaign certainly witnessed much greater involvement of technology, by both parties and voters. It would be stretching the truth, however, to state that it played a decisive role in the campaign. Each party had a website, and most of the candidates in individual constituencies had too. The Liberal Democrats were arguably the most innovative party in the use of the internet, offering a 'podcast' through their party's blog, and a virtual game whose purpose was to highlight more constructive ways to spend the money that the government had dedicated to the war in Iraq.

The two most popular sites during the campaign were hosted by BBC Online and Guardian Unlimited. They provided news, analysis and their own blogs on the campaign and were but two of hundreds of sites dedicated to some aspect of the election. Most were dedicated to providing opinion, but some attempted to have a direct bearing on the result in certain parts of the country. In some cases, this was by encouraging **tactical voting** (www.tacticalvoter.net) or by arranging the pairing of votes in neighbouring constituencies.

Overall, though, 2005 was not a breakthrough election for the internet. The failure of the main parties to encourage greater voter interaction on their sites, and the marginal nature of most blogs, meant that the opportunities for a genuine e-campaign were not fully exploited.

Task 4.1

(a) What do you understand by the term 'filter effect'?

(b) How has the influence of the media increased as a result of dealignment?

Task 4.1 (continued)

Guidance

(a) This is what voters automatically do to information that challenges their own political outlook. As a result, a voter is less likely to have his or her electoral preference shaped by the media.

(b) Dealignment has worked in two ways to increase the influence of the media. On one level it has acted on the *electorate*. With traditional loyalties weakened, voters are likely to be susceptible to different political influences. Although the short-term impact of the media is not thought to be particularly significant, over a prolonged period the media can have a decisive influence on voters. Dealignment can also be seen to have increased the impact of the media on *parties*. There is a certain amount of evidence to suggest that the Labour Party adopted policy positions on issues such as law and order and immigration to avoid hostile reactions from sections of the right-wing press. It has arguably also led to the party taking a more robust approach to news management, in the sense that it wants 'its' news to be presented in a favourable light by print and television journalists.

Turnout

Why does the level of turnout matter?

The United Kingdom is a parliamentary democracy, which allows its citizens to confer legitimacy on the government through regular elections. Elections therefore give a party a **mandate** to govern. If a significant minority of the population choose not to vote at all, not only does this undermine the right of the winning party to govern, but also it raises serious questions about the legitimacy of the political system as a whole. Two statistics from the last two elections provide an interesting comment on this issue:

- In 2001 more people chose *not* to vote than to vote on polling day.
- In 2005 the Labour government was elected with 35% of the electorate's support, from a turnout of 61%. That effectively means that its mandate to govern derives from barely a quarter of those registered to vote.

Who votes?

Turnout in 2005 was 61.4%, up 2% on the record low of 59.4% in 2001. It was the third lowest ever, and was 10% lower than it had been in 1997. According to the Electoral Commission, 17 million registered voters failed to visit a polling station on 5 May.

However, these figures hide considerable geographical disparities between constituencies throughout the UK, as Table 4.2 shows.

Table 4.2 High and low constituency turnouts in the 2005 general election

Top five constituency turnouts	%
West Tyrone	80.2
Fermanagh and South Tyrone	79.3
Mid Ulster	78.0
Newry and Armagh	76.3
West Dorset	76.2

Bottom five constituency turnouts	%
Liverpool Riverside	41.4
Manchester Central	43.1
Salford	43.3
Glasgow Central	44.1
Liverpool Walton	44.5

Source: the Electoral Commission

Note: technically, the postponed election in Staffordshire South saw the lowest turnout at 37.2%, but that took place several weeks after the national campaign had finished.

So, who is most likely to turn out to vote on polling day? Figure 4.3 gives some answers.

People who are most likely to vote (% turnout in 2005)

White (62%)
Aged 65+ (75%)
AB social group (70%)
Live in Northern Ireland (62.9%)
Live in a Conservative seat (65.5%)

Source: the Electoral Commission

People who are least likely to vote (% turnout in 2005)

Belong to an ethnic minority (47%)
Aged 18–24 (37%)
DE social group (54%)
Live in the North West (57.3%)
Live in a Labour seat (58%)

Figure 4.3 Characteristics of voters and non-voters

Why has turnout fallen during recent elections?

A quick examination of turnout levels reveals an alarming fall in the number of people voting in UK general elections. A combination of practical and theoretical explanations can be put forward to explain this phenomenon. Most of the survey data suggests that a tiny number of people are serial abstainers, while the majority of respondents in panel surveys attribute their failure to vote to practical reasons such as 'forgetting'.

Rational choice theory

Rational choice theory assumes that individuals calculate the costs and benefits of voting, and determine whether or not it is worth their effort to turn out on election day. In the first instance, this is a useful analytical tool for explaining why turnout is that much lower for what are known as **second-order elections** (see Figure 4.4). These are elections where the result does not directly affect how the country will be governed and are therefore regarded as less important than a **first-order election** such as the general election.

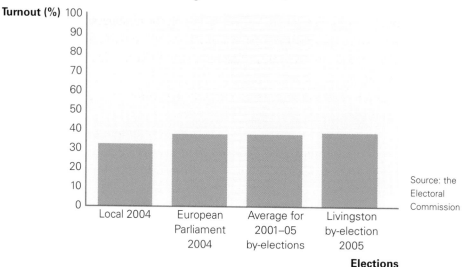

Source: the Electoral Commission

Figure 4.4 Turnout in recent UK second-order elections

As far as a general election is concerned, a voter would have to see the 'point' in voting. This might exist where the voter lives in a marginal constituency, where there would clearly be an incentive to express political preference. One could also point to voter concern about how the most important valence issues would be managed by each party: homeowners with a mortgage would certainly be keen to see a party in office that was capable of keeping interest rates down.

Rather like the 2001 election, survey data suggest that the electorate expected to see a comfortable Labour victory in 2005. In a poll published in *The Times* just prior to the election, 53% of respondents said that they believed Labour would win a 100-seat majority. If this indeed looked to be the case, many voters would feel that their vote was unlikely to count in another Labour landslide.

A comparison of turnout in marginal and safe seats also offers some support to the rational choice argument. In seats where the majority from 2001 was less than 5%, turnout was almost 67%. In safe seats, with a majority from 2001 of greater than 20%, turnout was 57%. This suggests that when voters feel that their vote 'counts', they will use it.

The stimulus effect

Another theory argues that low turnout is often the result of voters lacking a reason, or stimulus, to vote. Perhaps it is self-evident that voters with a strong identification with a party are more likely to vote, but obviously parties need to reach beyond their most loyal supporters if they are to win sufficient votes to gain power. However, research from recent elections suggests that one of the principal explanations for low turnout provided by non-voters was a failure by the political parties to provide sufficient reason to vote. This was attributable to several factors:

- There was a lack of knowledge about party platforms, and general ignorance about politics as a whole.
- Non-voters perceived that the parties offered very similar policies.
- The 4-week 2005 campaign failed to excite the electorate. The *Sun* referred to it as 'the most boring ever', while a MORI poll found that 49% of respondents disagreed with the view that it had been an interesting campaign.
- There was general cynicism about political parties, particularly the way in which they stage-managed events and offered spin at the expense of substance.
- Parties made little effort to meet voters. Relatively few of the electorate actually got to meet a candidate, with most parties targeting their attentions on the 800,000 voters in marginal seats, and even then relying mostly on mass leaflet drops instead of traditional door-to-door campaigning.

One reason why the stimulus effect is relevant in explaining differences in turnout levels is that the older generation, who are more likely to vote, require less external incentive to vote. In a British Election Study survey conducted after the 2005 election, over 90% of the 65+ group said that they agreed with the view that voting was a civic duty, compared to 56% of 18–24-year-olds.

Social location

Finally, a person's social location can also have an impact. That is to say, factors such as age, ethnic group and class can determine whether a person is likely to vote.

Age

Whereas older generations tend to feel a sense of civic duty where voting is concerned, younger voters are less likely to feel such a responsibility and may also question the relevance of voting, and politics in general, to their lives.

Ethnic group

While different patterns exist between minority ethnic groups, their relatively low level of enthusiasm for voting can partially be explained by a lack of engagement with the political process. With relatively few candidates from ethnic minorities standing for election, one could argue that those from minority ethnic communities may feel little attachment to politics in the UK.

Class

Voters living in inner-city areas are more likely to move around and may therefore no longer be in the place where they are registered to vote. One theory to explain why voters on low income, with low levels of education and with poor health are more likely to abstain is that they feel removed from normal political and community networks. That is to say, none of the parties offers any real hope for their lives to be improved.

How can falling turnout be addressed?

A number of mechanisms have been devised to arrest the trend towards declining turnout.

Postal voting

Although postal voting was already available for a small section of the electorate, such as those on holiday or in the armed forces, the restrictions on postal voting were considerably relaxed prior to the 2001 election. In 2005 12% of all votes were cast by post. (Interestingly, 5 million postal votes were sent out to voters, but only 4 million were returned.)

Postal vote — John Prescott sets the example

The effect on turnout appears to have been slight — after all, overall turnout in 2005 only increased by 2% on 2001. However, perhaps the best way to examine the impact of the postal vote would be to consider how far turnout increased in those constituencies that saw the biggest increase in postal voting. Here the results appear to be inconclusive, as Figure 4.5 shows.

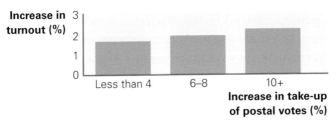

Figure 4.5 Postal voting and increased turnout, 2001–05

Arguably postal voting will have a greater effect on turnout in second-order elections. In 2004 local authorities in the North East, North West, Yorkshire and the Humber and the East Midlands conducted all-postal ballots, while in other areas, where the postal vote was optional, 8.6% of the electorate applied for a postal ballot for the local and European elections. Turnout in both the local and European Parliament elections was higher as a result of postal voting. In the local elections, turnout was up 10% on the previous year, while the turnout of 38% was the highest ever for European Parliament elections.

The general election of 2005 focused attention on one weakness in the current system of postal voting: party involvement in applications for a postal vote (see Box 4.4).

Box 4.4

Postal voting irregularities, 2005

- A Labour supporter in Birmingham was found to have redirected postal ballots for friends to his house.
- In Bradford two men were arrested on suspicion of postal voting fraud.
- Police investigations also took place in Leicester East, Leicester South, Bethnal Green & Bow, High Wycombe, Luton, Southampton and Somerset & Frome.
- Three men were charged with defrauding the electoral system in Burnley.
- Voters in Oldham and Basingstoke were sent duplicate ballot papers.

The government is currently reviewing the use of postal voting in future elections, with likely reforms to include removing serial numbers from ballot papers and stopping the practice of applications being completed by the head of household. Already in March 2006 the three main parties signed up to a code of conduct aimed at limiting the role of candidates and canvassers in helping

voters to complete the postal ballot paper and in handling completed postal ballot papers.

e-voting

In 2002, the government unveiled an action plan, including pilot schemes, to allow an 'electronically enabled' general election to take place after 2006. However, these plans, which would have included provision for voting by text message and the internet in the 2006 local elections, were scrapped by the government in September 2005. Indeed, after the government launched its action plan, it faced mounting criticism over its e-voting project. Concerns were expressed about the anonymity and security of voting, and even the trust-worthiness of internet service providers. It has also been argued by Professor Stephen Coleman of the Oxford Internet Institute that increasing the convenience of voting will not tackle the more fundamental problems of non-voting, such as disengagement with the political process.

Electronic voting has been used in several countries already, although its effectiveness has been questioned. Several US states have used e-voting since the start of the decade, and Spain, India, Australia and Costa Rica have also experimented with it. The Republic of Ireland introduced e-voting for three out of 42 constituencies in its 2002 general election, before cancelling plans to extend its use to the 2004 European Parliament elections.

More accessible polling stations

In May 2003, Swindon, Sheffield and 16 other boroughs experienced the first council elections to feature mobile voting. Residents of care homes or sheltered accommodation had the 'ballot box' brought to their door. Polling kiosks were positioned in convenient parts of the city and voters could even vote from home. Residents of remote areas in Australia have enjoyed similar experiences for several years.

Increasing voter registration

In September 2005, the Electoral Commission revealed that 3.7 million people who were eligible to vote had not registered to do so in 2005. The lack of registration is greatest among non-white ethnic groups in the UK. Whereas 6% of white people were unregistered, over 17% of ethnic minority groups had not registered. A similar number of 18–24-year-olds had also failed to do so.

One explanation for the numbers of unregistered is the way that households register to vote. At present, the head of the household completes the registration. The commission would like a system of individual registration to be introduced.

Addressing voter apathy

A common criticism from those who oppose simply making it more convenient to vote is that the prime cause of low turnout is voter apathy. This could result from a lack of real choice at the ballot box, or from people being put off by the confrontational style in which politics is conducted in the UK.

In order to reinvigorate the political process, it is argued, parties need to reach out to voters more. Research carried out on behalf of the Electoral Commission into voter attitudes during the 2004 European Parliament election campaign suggested that, by raising the profile of an election, the parties can have a direct bearing on turnout. The research found that a wider distribution of campaign material led voters to identify differences between the parties. If this had been done in 2004, it could have led to the highest ever European Parliament election turnout in the UK.

Compulsory voting

Any voter in Australia, Austria, Belgium and Greece who fails to turn out on polling day can expect to be punished. In Australia, this involves a fine of A$50; in Belgium, non-voters can be excluded from the electoral register for 10 years.

Currently, voting is a voluntary act in the UK, but Geoff Hoon, the leader of the House of Commons, has advocated making it compulsory. His proposal would also enable voters to tick a box for 'none of the above', maintaining the right of electors to abstain.

> International experience points to compulsory voting being the most effective way to increase turnout.
>
> Geoff Hoon, 2005

Opinion polls

Opinion polls have been a feature of general election campaigns since the mid-1960s. Parties rely heavily on them to gauge which messages are playing well with the electorate, media outlets use them to provide their angle on the campaign, and voters use them to plot the likely fortunes of the parties. As far as the impact on the campaign is concerned, though, their real significance lies first in their accuracy, and second in their role not just in demonstrating voter opinion, but in actually influencing it.

How accurate are opinion polls?

Having the ability to produce accurate polls is essential if polling companies are to be commissioned by agencies, parties and the media to survey public

opinion. As far as election campaigns are concerned, polls have to be able to plot accurately the direction of voters during the course of the campaign and to predict the eventual result in their exit poll, usually taken on the day of polling. Accuracy is gauged by examining the mean difference between each party's share of the exit poll and the actual election result.

Since 1970, the pollsters have, for the most part, enjoyed considerable success in predicting the winning party and the extent of support that they would receive. Polling companies allow a margin of error of +/−3%, which allows for discrepancies in the sample, postal voting and fluctuations in turnout. The biggest problem that pollsters have had historically is with the size of Labour's share of the vote. A recurring problem is a tendency to overestimate Labour's actual performance, something which led the pollsters to get the result of the 1992 election wrong: four out of the five exit polls gave Labour a narrow lead, suggesting a hung parliament. The Conservatives actually got 7.6% more than Labour, giving them 5 more years in office.

Even after polling techniques were refined after 1992, Labour's share of the vote in 1997 and 2001 was still 4–5% lower than was predicted during the campaign. In both cases, this was of little significance, as Labour enjoyed huge majorities, but if the actual result had been closer, then the polls could have had a decisive effect on the eventual result.

Task 4.2

Study the final opinion polls from the 2005 campaign shown in Table 4.3.

Table 4.3 Final opinion polls and actual result in the 2005 general election

Poll	Conservatives (%)	Labour (%)	Liberal Democrats (%)
Communicate Research	31	39	23
ICM	32	38	22
NOP	33	36	23
Populus	32	38	21
YouGov	32	37	24
MORI	33	38	23
Result	33	36	23

Source: P. Norris and C. Wlezien (eds), *Britain Votes 2005* (2005)

(a) How far do the errors of previous campaigns appear to have been removed?

(b) What factors undermine the effectiveness of polls in predicting the number of seats that each party will have after the election?

Task 4.2 (continued)

Guidance

(a) The polling companies can take some comfort from their performance in 2005, with every exit poll falling well within the accepted margin of error. NOP actually managed to predict the actual result correctly. However, the tendency to over-estimate the likely level of Labour support was still present, with Communicate Research being 3 percentage points out.

(b) Several factors can undermine their effectiveness. They rely primarily on respondents providing honest answers. Late swings in the last few days of the campaign can make the polls look inaccurate, as happened in 1992. The composition of the sample might not be representative of the electorate as a whole. The workings of the electoral system might also further complicate things, with polls being unable to take into account local patterns, tactical voting or the bias towards Labour.

To what extent do opinion polls influence voting behaviour?

How far polls can actually influence an election result is open to debate. In recent elections, they could be seen to have had a positive and a negative impact on party performance, as shown in Box 4.5.

Box 4.5

Opinion polls: positive and negative effects

Positive

- Some commentators refer to a 'bandwagon effect' taking place, where voters switch their allegiance to a party that looks like it is doing well in the polls. They might do so where their 'natural' allegiance is to a minor party that is exceeding expectations, or simply because a herd mentality kicks in.
- Polls can also encourage voters to vote tactically. Each of the parties makes widespread use of local polling to persuade floating voters that they can make a real difference to the result. The Liberal Democrats made great play of the fact that Labour could not win in Cheadle in 2005, thus encouraging Labour supporters to vote tactically in order to defeat the Conservative candidate.

Negative

- Where a result looks a foregone conclusion, opinion polls can depress turnout. This might explain why turnout was considerably lower in safe Labour seats in

---

> Box 4.5 (continued)
>
> 1997, 2001 and 2005. In each case, the polls forecast a large Labour majority. Given that Labour's core voters among the young and less well-off are less likely to vote in the first place, knowing that their party was going to win anyway deprived them of the required stimulus to vote.
> - Polls can also have the effect of turning voters away from a party that appears to be running away with the election. It has already been established that the polls traditionally exaggerate Labour's likely share of the vote, and there is some evidence that this prompted waverers to switch from Labour in 2001 and 2005.

Conclusion: how important was the campaign in 2005?

After spending in excess of £50 million on the 2005 election campaign, did the parties get their money's worth? At first glance, the answer has to be no. The opinion polls registered very little change in voter intention, or willingness, to vote from the date the election was called to 5 May. The predicted outcome occurred — a Labour victory — as did the expected 'bloody nose' given to Tony Blair by the electorate. Post-election survey data provide a significant clue to why the campaign produced such a predictable result: the vast majority of voters had made up their mind how they were going to vote before the start of the campaign.

Much of the evidence also suggests that the campaign failed to act as a stimulus to those groups in society who are most reluctant to vote. Interestingly, a MORI poll in April 2005 found that 61% of respondents were 'absolutely certain' to vote, and a further 19% indicated that they were more likely to vote than not. The actual turnout, as we know, was considerably less than the combined total of 80%. These figures might suggest that the campaign actually served to deter people from voting.

However, this general picture ignores two important aspects of the impact of election campaigns. First, there is ample evidence that points to a significant *local* impact of election campaigns. Differences in swings throughout the country and some very peculiar election-night results, such as the Liberal Democrat John Leech taking Manchester Withington from a longstanding Labour MP, indicate that not all constituencies are immune to intensive campaigning.

Second, this election campaign was only 4 weeks, out of a much longer political battle. The Conservative election campaign had arguably started twice before already: once when Iain Duncan Smith was elected leader of the party, and again when he was replaced by Michael Howard, who led the party into the election proper. Everything that the parties did or said during the official campaign has to be placed into a longer-term context; their messages and key personnel remained constant for at least the previous year, and in many cases since the previous election.

Task 4.3

Read the following comments made by voters in 2005 and answer the questions that follow.

Source A

'We got voting papers for three people who moved out over 6 months ago. It didn't matter that I'd told the council that when I applied to be added to the electoral roll. Apparently since these three haven't applied elsewhere, they'll still be on the electoral roll for my house until they do.'

Source B

'I think the postal votes system is a disgrace — I had 32 votes registered to my house and even then I wasn't able to ensure victory for my preferred candidate!'

(a) In what ways do both these sources indicate problems with postal voting in the 2005 election?

(b) Certain regions have already experimented with all-postal voting for local elections. What are the main arguments against this?

Guidance

(a) Source A indicates that the electoral roll is still too inflexible to keep apace of changes of residence. This effectively disenfranchises the person in this source until the previous residents register to vote elsewhere. Source B highlights administrative problems that have arisen in the past, with individuals able to make multiple votes, due to clerical errors.

(b) The main arguments against postal voting include:
- It undermines the principle of the secret ballot, as forms require the signature of a witness.
- This could increase voter intimidation if party officials continue to act as witnesses to postal voters.
- Cases of electoral fraud could increase in number, with voters registering false addresses or forging signatures.

Task 4.3 (continued)

- Registration and completion of the ballot papers is still the responsibility of the head of household. In theory, this could place several votes in the hands of one individual.
- Its extension to the whole electorate will do nothing to tackle deep-rooted causes of low turnout.

Useful websites

- MORI
  www.mori.com
  and, for the results of opinion polls between 1992 and 2005:
  www.mori.com/polls/trends/voting-allpub-trends.shtml#2005
- BBC NEWS
  http://news.bbc.co.uk
  and, for the results of opinion polls between January and 5 May 2005:
  http://news.bbc.co.uk/1/shared/vote2005/polltracker/html/polltracker.stm
- Political Science Resources
  www.psr.keele.ac.uk
  and, for information on the 2005 general election:
  www.psr.keele.ac.uk/area/uk/ge05.htm

Further reading

- Lynch, P. (2002) 'Goodbye ballot box, hello post box', *Talking Politics*, vol. 15, no. 1.
- Wild, E. (2003) 'Modern myths of electoral apathy', *Talking Politics*, vol. 16, no. 1.

How important are referendums in UK politics?

Critics of representative democracy argue that reliance on mandate theory to guarantee the right of a party to govern ignores several critical weaknesses in this form of democracy. Arguably the most important is the limited opportunity it provides for the electorate to participate in the political process. It also assumes that voters support the entire package of policies that a party presents in its manifesto. It is unlikely that many voters are aware of the various policy positions of their preferred party, and it is equally unlikely that they support the positions of their party on every issue. In a country such as Switzerland, these problems are partially resolved through regular recourse to initiatives. However, until relatively recently, politicians in the UK have been reluctant to place their trust in popular opinion.

This chapter focuses on the growing importance of referendums in the UK. It examines the reason why referendums are called, considers their many advantages and disadvantages, and suggests reasons why they have become a more common feature of UK political life.

What are referendums?

Referendums ask voters a single question on a specific issue, and usually require a simple yes/no response. An example of this is the question asked in the only national referendum in the UK to date:

Do you think that the UK should remain in the EEC?

This question was put to the UK electorate in June 1975, with 67.2% of those who voted saying 'yes'.

Although referendums generally require a yes/no response, they can differ from each other in several ways. As indicated in Chapter 1, some referendums

can be called by the electorate. These are commonly referred to as initiatives. The purpose of referendums can also differ in the sense that some may only be used to gauge public opinion on a particular issue (these are referred to as **indicative referendums**), whereas ones that will actually lead to legislative change are known as **binding referendums**. These are often held *after* the legislation has been passed by the legislature — the purpose of the referendum is effectively to provide popular ratification.

Learning point

Binding or indicative?

The New Zealand government has held two referendums on reforming its electoral system. In 1992 an indicative referendum was held, with 85% of voters expressing a desire to change the electoral system. A binding referendum was held the following year, with the result that the country's FPTP system was replaced by an AMS-style mixed member system.

What circumstances might prompt a government to hold an indicative rather than a binding referendum?

In order to ensure that a 'yes' vote genuinely signifies popular support for a measure, some governments insist on a threshold being reached before the motion is carried. An example of such a threshold being used in UK politics is the 1979 referendum on Scottish and Welsh devolution. English Labour MPs inserted a clause into the respective Scotland and Wales Acts insisting that at least 40% of the electorate should vote for devolution. As Task 5.2 illustrates, this ensured the failure of the government's plans in Scotland, while pro-devolutionists in Wales, angry at the limited nature of the devolution plans, joined with opponents of the measure to provide a definite 'no' to the referendum question. A different kind of threshold exists in Italy, where 50% of the electorate have to participate for the referendum to be legal. Some referendums allow voters to express a preference between several alternatives. The 1993 referendum on New Zealand's electoral system offered a choice of alternatives to the existing FPTP system.

Why do governments hold referendums?

Governments hold referendums for several reasons.

To legitimise constitutional changes

The use of a referendum to legitimise constitutional changes has been found in many states, and has been behind the majority of those held in the UK, Ireland, New Zealand, Australia, France and several US states. Local and regional referendums held in the UK since 1997 have been based on a range of proposed constitutional measures, and the government has promised to hold referendums on other constitutional areas at some point in the future (see Figure 5.1).

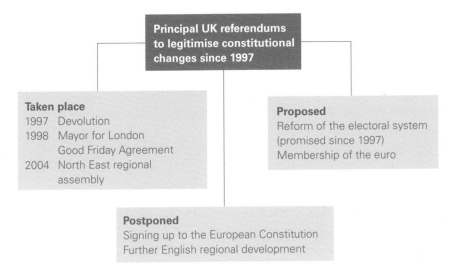

Principal UK referendums to legitimise constitutional changes since 1997

Taken place
1997 Devolution
1998 Mayor for London
     Good Friday Agreement
2004 North East regional
     assembly

Proposed
Reform of the electoral system
(promised since 1997)
Membership of the euro

Postponed
Signing up to the European Constitution
Further English regional development

Figure 5.1 Constitutional referendums in the UK

To entrench constitutional changes

There are obviously links here to the previous reason. Not only can governments claim a legitimate right to amend the constitution if the matter has been put to a popular vote, but they can effectively entrench this reform in the same way. For example, the only way to reverse devolution in Scotland and Wales is through a further referendum — a stipulation that would prevent a hostile government in England from abolishing either legislature, and that arguably fire-proofed the Scottish Parliament and Welsh Assembly during their difficult first few years.

To settle complex ethical and moral issues

Referendums can be a useful political tool for governments in countries with a strong religious tradition. Where a tension exists between reformist secular groups and a religious organisation, the referendum can offer a means of settling controversial social issues. This has particularly been the case in Catholic

countries such as Ireland and Portugal. In 1998, a vote to legalise abortion was narrowly defeated 51–49% in Portugal. In September 2005, the Portuguese parliament voted to allow a second referendum on this issue, but this was struck down by the country's constitutional court a month later.

Allowing politicians and voters a free vote, without a responsibility to vote along party lines, can also prevent an issue from becoming a means of scoring political points.

To overcome political disunity

UK party politics is characterised by its adversarial nature and the requirement to maintain an impression of party unity. Occasionally, an issue comes along that threatens to divide a ruling party and could potentially destabilise an otherwise secure administration. In this context, the referendum can provide a means of tolerating significant internal dissent, while allowing opposing groups to make their case to the country.

The classic example of this in UK politics is the 1975 vote on continued membership of the EEC. Prime Minister Harold Wilson, aware of the deep division that existed in the Labour Party over Europe, and hoping to exploit similar Tory splits, included a commitment to a referendum in Labour's October 1974 manifesto. The ensuing campaign saw inter-party division submerged as pro-EEC Tories and Labour politicians shared the same political platform.

Why have referendums been used more regularly since 1997?

Historically, the referendum has not been a regular method of making policy in the UK. There has only ever been one national referendum: the 1975 question on continued membership of the EEC. However, since the election of New Labour, the referendum has become a much more regularly used political device, with five regional and over 30 local referendums already having taken place, and with plans for three more at a national level.

The willingness of Tony Blair's government to revert to referendums can be explained by a combination of factors.

First, many of the issues central to Labour's agenda since 1997 have involved a redistribution of power within the UK. One of Labour's 'big ideas' when it came to power was a radical overhaul of the constitution. This included reform of the House of Lords, electoral reform, devolution, incorporation of the European Convention of Human Rights, elected mayors, local cabinets and regional devolution. Labour could certainly have relied on its huge parliamentary majorities to implement these measures, and indeed did so with the 1998 Human Rights Act, which incorporated the European Convention on Human Rights into UK law. However, in spite of the motives behind them, the 1975 and 1979 referendums had established a precedent that issues of this nature ought to be put before the public.

Second, the new government inherited one very specific and delicate problem from the outgoing Conservative administration: the peace process in Northern Ireland. The Good Friday Agreement, signed in April 1998, was a compromise package that ended the first stage of the peace process. Faced with two distinct political communities that shared a history of intractable hostility, the 22 May 1998 referendum proved to be a unique political experience in the province, with both unionist and nationalist/republican communities providing majority support for the establishment of a new

Good Friday Agreement referendum — Seamus Mallon and John Hume of the SDLP on 23 May 1998

devolved system of government. The position of the British government, over the course of many administrations, was that the principle of popular consent would govern any changes to the relationship between the Northern Ireland and the mainland. The referendum provided that consent and tied both sides in the conflict to the terms of the agreement.

One interesting feature of this particular referendum was that the citizens of another country, the Republic of Ireland, also voted on the issue at the same time.

Third, one could make the case that the regular use of the referendum by Tony Blair is entirely consistent with a style of government that places great emphasis on frequent gauging of popular opinion. Reliance on people's panels, focus groups and citizens' juries have become an established characteristic of New Labour in power. One of Blair's closest political allies outlined the link between the use of referendums and the changing nature of representative government in March 1998.

Tony Blair's government has already held two referendums and three more are at some stage in prospect, not to mention more citizens' movements, more action from pressure groups.

Representative government is being complemented by more direct forms of involvement from the internet to referendums. This requires a different style of politics and we are trying to respond to these changes.

Peter Mandelson, Minister without Portfolio, 1998

The government White Paper 'Local Democracy and Community Leadership' (1997) outlined various ways in which local politics could be reinvigorated through greater public participation. The ensuing Local Government Act 2000 provided councils with the authority to put a wide range of issues, including the level of council tax increase, before the electorate.

Finally, short-term political considerations have also played their part. Prior to the 1997 general election, the Labour leadership was concerned about the party's vulnerability on two key issues:

- Where future UK membership of the euro was concerned, the party was under threat from a Conservative Party that had already pledged itself to a referendum on the issue, and from Sir James Goldsmith's Referendum Party, which promised to put UK membership of the EU to a nationwide vote. Anxious not to appear more euro-friendly and less democratic than either of the two other parties, Gordon Brown committed Labour to securing popular consent before abandoning the pound.
- The second issue revolved around the possibility of a future devolved Scottish Parliament possessing tax-raising powers. This controversial proposal threatened to undermine the party's image as a fiscally prudent, economically sound alternative to the Conservatives. By referring final judgement to the Scottish electorate, Blair and Brown managed to defuse a potentially damaging political issue.

A further example of realpolitik dictating government attitudes towards referendums was provided in April 2004, when the prime minister announced to the House of Commons that a future referendum would be held in the UK to ratify the new European Constitution. With very little justification for the referendum forthcoming, commentators were left to speculate as to the government's motives. There was certainly an issue about the possible effects on UK sovereignty of signing up to the constitution, but this would not explain why the vote had been announced at that point, nor why there had not been a vote on either the Amsterdam or Nice treaties, both of which impacted more greatly upon UK sovereignty and were the subject of referendums in most other EU member states. However, the authors of *Monitor*, a journal of the Constitution Unit based at University College London, have argued that the main considerations were party political. They suggest that Blair feared a revolt in the House of Lords, where an amendment might be passed to the ratification bill insisting on a referendum on the issue. At the same time, likely public opposition to the constitution was signalled by Labour's poor performance in the June 2004 European Parliament elections, won by a euro-sceptical Conservative Party.

Task 5.1

Examine Table 5.1 and answer the questions that follow.

Table 5.1 Themes of recent referendums in the UK

Date	Issue	Result
September 1997	Scottish devolution	Yes
	Tax-raising powers for a Scottish Parliament	Yes
	Welsh devolution	Yes
May 1998	Creation of a London Mayor and Assembly	Yes
	Good Friday Agreement, Northern Ireland	Yes
February 2001	Whether council tax in Bristol should increase	No
September 2001	Creation of an elected Mayor for Doncaster	Yes
November 2004	North East regional assembly	No

(a) What light do the data in the table throw on the reasons why referendums are held in the UK?

(b) How far have the referendums in the table undermined representative democracy in the UK?

Guidance

(a) The table suggests that referendums are used predominantly for constitutional matters, such as devolution, but also to bind a divided community to a political decision, as with the vote on the Good Friday Agreement. The council tax vote in Bristol could be interpreted as a way of compensating for a lack of political will on behalf of the ruling group.

(b) They have undermined representative democracy by removing decisions from parliamentary control and passing them to the mass electorate. Where devolution in Scotland and Wales is concerned, they have ensured that the constitutional future of both regions will be decided by referendums, not parliament. The Bristol case might set a dangerous precedent whereby politicians abdicate responsibility where an unpopular decision is required.

An argument against this view is that the referendums actually complement representative democracy by removing sensitive decisions from accusations of party political bias. Parliament also played a significant role in devolution by debating and passing legislative acts, which only became law after the successful referendums.

Assessing the value of referendums

The value of referendums can be gauged by considering their advantages and disadvantages.

What are the advantages of referendums?

They increase popular participation in decision making

From the point of view of an individual voter, one vote every 5 years is scant opportunity to influence policy making in the UK directly, so referendums are another chance to have a say in politics.

Somebody living in Hartlepool since 1997 would have had the opportunity to participate in the decision-making processes shown in Figure 5.2. While it might appear that the Hartlepool voter has had only two extra votes, this is two more than a similar voter living in the North West, where there has been no local referendum during the same period and where plans for a regional referendum were scrapped in 2004.

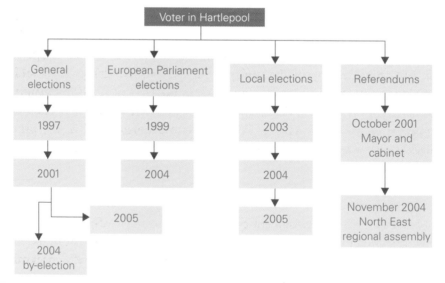

Figure 5.2 Opportunities for voter participation in Hartlepool, 1997–2005

Using referendums more could also rejuvenate a political system that appears to have lost the confidence of its citizens. Advocates of the greater use of referendums would argue that decisions are best taken out of the hands of ruling elites and should instead be in the hands of the people. This argument has recently been deployed by some supporters of further European integration, in an attempt to rebuild confidence in decision-making procedures.

Learning point
Rebuilding the EU

I think that forms of direct democracy are necessary as an iron bar. Besides choosing the chairman of the European Commission, a European rejective referendum and a European popular initiative are important weapons for the citizens. In theory, this could now and then lead to a setback. But it would amount to arrogance to build a political union upon a half-functioning democracy.

Dick Benschop, secretary of European affairs, Netherlands government,
Vrij Nederland, 12 May 2001

Do you agree with the view that failing to hold referendums leads to a 'half-functioning democracy'?

In Switzerland, the use of the **facultative referendum** gives the electorate the potential to amend any federal law so long as 50,000 people petition for it. In doing so, it offers an interesting compromise between outright direct democracy and parliamentary democracy.

They overcome flaws in the mandate theory

One of the major flaws in mandate theory is that it assumes voters agree with all the policies of the party they vote for. As has been demonstrated elsewhere, voters tend to base their electoral preferences more on generalised images than on a detailed scrutiny of the different manifestos. Inevitably, this could be argued to undermine the mandate model, as the electorate has not genuinely approved specific party policies. By holding regular referendums, representative democracies would be able to overcome this problem, and in the process provide greater legitimacy for the government's actions.

They provide a definitive answer to a politically sensitive or complex issue

Parties may think that certain issues are too delicate to be left to MPs, who may feel compelled to vote along party lines, or will feel able to overturn the legislation in future parliaments. In other cases, ethnic or religious influences might determine the direction of their vote.

Perhaps the best demonstration of this advantage of referendums in recent UK political history was the referendum on the Good Friday Agreement in May 1998. This was consistent with the UK government's policy of consent and ensured that all sections of the community were tied into the peace process. Stipulating that a majority of unionists and a majority of nationalists had to vote 'yes', the government was able to provide a definitive, binding answer to the question of Northern Ireland's future political direction.

The 2005 vote on the Iraqi Constitution presents an interesting alternative example of when a popular vote is held in these circumstances. Believing that ethnic divisions and political rivalry would undermine any coalition-imposed political settlement, the US civilian administrator in Iraq drew up the question:

Do you approve of the draft constitution of Iraq?

Designed to unite all sections of Iraqi society, the referendum paved the way for elections to be held for a new Iraqi assembly and the move towards an independent nation-state.

They offer voters an alternative to political parties with similar policies

According to its founder, Sir James Goldsmith, one of the main reasons for the creation of the Referendum Party was the alleged lack of choice presented by the main political parties on the issue of UK membership of the European Union in general, and joining the single currency in particular. This effectively deprived voters of selecting a party that opposed further European integration.

His intention was ultimately to present UK citizens with a referendum on these issues, along the lines of two questions:

Sir James Goldsmith

Do you want the United Kingdom to be part of a Federal Europe?
Do you want the United Kingdom to return to an association of sovereign states that are part of a common trading market?

They serve a valuable citizenship function by educating voters about political issues

A by-product of referendum campaigns is increased political awareness. Saturated with literature and news coverage, voters cannot help but take notice of the main arguments surrounding an issue. This can have important social consequences too. In October 2005 the Brazilian government held a vote on the continued sale of firearms in the country. Although the result was in favour of the continued sale of firearms, it was felt that the referendum formed a useful part of the government's 'Project Disarmament' against high levels of violence in Brazil.

A similar argument was used to justify the Iraqi referendum. Simply by getting ordinary people to engage in the political process, in many cases for the first time, its architects believed that they were taking an important step towards the construction of a democratic political state.

They enable the executive to appeal directly to the electorate over the heads of an obstructive parliament

The circumstances in which this may take place are likely to include a government with a narrow parliamentary majority, or with a parliamentary institution, such as the House of Lords, that might block the passage of a piece of legislation. A government wishing to introduce a new method of electing MPs would be unlikely to get sufficient support from a legislature whose members might fear losing their seats under an alternative system.

It can also apply where relations between central and local government are strained. In 2003 the local government minister Nick Raynsford threatened to use local referendums as a way of capping council tax increases in England, effectively appealing to voters over the heads of local councils.

They can prevent parties from dividing over a single issue

While critics of referendums might present this as an undesirable use of referendums, one can make the point that repeated splintering of political parties might bring with it equally undesirable political instability. In the case of the Conservative Party, putting an issue such as the euro to a referendum might enable it to concentrate on providing an effective opposition to Labour and, in the process, present the electorate with a clearer choice of future government.

What are the disadvantages of referendums?

They undermine the principle of parliamentary sovereignty

The principle of parliamentary sovereignty could be affected in two ways. First, the ultimate responsibility for making legislation would pass to the electorate. Second, the right of parliament to repeal previous legislation would also be undermined, as a post-legislation referendum could lead to the legislation being removed from the statute book, as happened with the 1978 Scotland Act, after the government lost the 1979 referendum.

The result can be influenced by the wording of the question

Asking whether voters wish to see an increase in their council taxes, or whether they want to see schools and hospitals close, could make an enormous difference to how people vote. Although the Electoral Commission has the power to pass comment on the wording of questions, it lacks the power to make its recommendations binding on the government. For the proposed referendums on regional assemblies, the government included, where geographically relevant, a second complicated question on creating a single tier of local

government. This was in spite of the fact that the commission regarded this as too complicated for voters.

Learning point

Government neutrality?

During the North East regional assembly referendum, the director of the 'no' campaign had this to say about the monitoring of the campaign:

> The problems of the Electoral Commission are too numerous to go into…nobody should be under any illusion that the commission exists to police conduct at referenda. When we complained [about government interference in the campaign], it said there was nothing it could do.

(a) Do you think that governments should remain neutral during referendum campaigns?
(b) How could restrictions on government activity be enforced?

Democratic motives do not always influence the decision to call a referendum

The history of referendums in the UK shows that they are frequently used to serve political self-interest rather than the cause of increased popular participation. Harold Wilson's motives in 1975 have already been mentioned, but New Labour has been equally willing to abuse referendums. More recently, the Bristol referendum in 2001 was prompted by the ruling Labour group, which was reluctant to lose control of the council by having to make a choice between, on the one hand, raising council taxes and risking alienating voters, and on the other, keeping them static and having to trim public services — something likely to lead to a split in the local Labour Party.

As explained above, Tony Blair's approach to the European Constitution also betrays a lack of conviction in direct democratic methods.

Low turnouts undermine the legitimacy of the result and can lead to a 'tyranny of the minority'

Turnout for the 1998 referendum on a mayor for London was 34.1%, with the figure falling to around 25% in some parts of Greater London. The 'yes' campaign achieved an overwhelming majority of the vote (72%), but the decision to change the way London was governed was approved by only 24% of registered voters. While many countries insist on a minimum turnout threshold, this has never been the case in any of the referendums held in mainland Britain since 1997. Before the vote on a regional assembly for the North East, the government said that it would not accept a result that had a derisory turnout. However, it did not specify what it meant by 'derisory'.

Inequalities in funding can unduly influence the final result

Evidence from the 1997 Welsh devolution campaign and various referendums on European integration point to the significant impact that a clear financial advantage can have on the result. In Ireland, the successful government-backed 'yes' campaign for the second vote on ratifying the Nice Treaty outspent the 'no' campaign by a ratio of 20:1. Although the Electoral Commission has laid down strict rules regarding the funding and expenditure levels of future referendum campaigns, the government could still use public money to make its case before the official start of the campaign (even though this would conflict with the 1998 Neill Report recommendation that the government should remain neutral).

In 2000 Brian Souter, a Scottish businessman, demonstrated the effect that a wealthy individual can have on referendum results. As part of his campaign to prevent the Scottish Parliament repealing the controversial Section 28 of the Local Government Act 1988, Mr Souter financed his own private referendum on the issue. Spending approximately £500,000 on the campaign brought him the backing of 87% of those who voted. Turnout, however, was only 34%.

Some political issues are too complex for a referendum

In the first instance, a referendum usually requires a complex political issue to be reduced to a simple yes/no format. This obviously fails to take into account subtle differences of opinion and rules out compromise settlements. The 1973 question 'Should Northern Ireland remain part of the UK?' provides a clear example of this problem. In this case, the answer would depend on the arrangements made for Northern Ireland to remain in the UK. Voters would need the answers to questions on the relationship between the province and the mainland and the rights that nationalists would enjoy before making their preference known.

A popular vote might also be influenced by powerful individuals or groups, who could provide a simplified or distorted view of the issues to a politically illiterate electorate. Instead, argue supporters of representative democracy, complex decisions should be left to well-informed specialists — that is, to MPs.

The electorate does not vote on the issue, but treats the referendum as an opinion poll on the government

This is particularly the case when a party has been in power for a considerable period of time, or the economy is in a recession. The case of Denmark's 1993 referendum on the Maastricht Treaty, when the Danish prime minister had been in power for 10 years, supports this view, as does the fact that the 2000 vote on joining the euro failed at a time when the Danish prime minister was accused of breaking several election promises.

Referendums can be instruments of authoritarian rule

Historically, referendums have been associated with political leaders who wanted to gain a personal mandate for their policies from the country as a whole. Hitler held two referendums, in 1934 and in 1938, while post-communist leaders in eastern Europe have also realised the benefits of popular sovereignty.

Conclusion: how important are referendums in UK politics?

Referendums have become a regular feature of political life in the UK. Although no national poll has taken place since 1975, voters throughout the UK have been exposed to the workings of direct democracy at regional, county or town level. These have required popular decisions on issues as diverse as levels of taxation and whether Edinburgh should introduce its own version of the congestion charge. However, the government is still very unwilling to interfere with the traditional prerogative of parliament to decide on most domestic and foreign political issues, and shows no sign of placing ethical or social issues before the electorate. Ultimately, the lack of established constitutional guidelines for the use of referendums, as exists in Italy, Switzerland and many other European states, ensures that a significant degree of scepticism remains about the role of referendums in the UK. For this reason alone, they cannot yet be classed as an important feature of UK political life.

Task 5.2

In the 1979 referendums on Scottish and Welsh devolution, English Labour MPs inserted a clause in the legislation insisting that 40% of the total electorate (not just those who voted) had to vote 'yes' for the proposal to advance. The results are given in Table 5.2.

Table 5.2 Results of the Scottish and Welsh devolution referendums, 1979

	Yes	No
Scotland	51.5% (32.8% of the electorate)	48.5%
Wales	20.3% (11.9% of the electorate)	79.7%

Task 5.2 (continued)

No such threshold existed in 1997. Voters in Scotland and Wales merely had to provide a majority of support for the government's devolution proposals (voters in Scotland were also asked if they wanted a parliament with tax-raising powers). The 1997 results are given in Table 5.3.

Table 5.3 Results of the Scottish and Welsh devolution referendums, 1997

	Yes	No
Scotland	74.3% (44.7% of the electorate)	25.7%
Tax-raising powers for the Scottish Parliament	63.5%	36.5%
Wales	50.3% (25.2% of the electorate)	49.7%

(a) Why were referendums used to ratify these devolution measures?

(b) In what ways do the results illustrate the weakness of the referendum as a decision-making tool?

Guidance

(a) As a major constitutional issue, affecting the relationship between the people of the regions and their rulers, devolution is an obvious choice for a referendum. In both cases, political reasons also influenced the decision to put them to a popular vote. In 1978 the Labour government lacked the will and parliamentary support to pass the measure through parliament, but was trapped by its need to maintain the support of nationalist parties in the Commons. In 1997 Tony Blair's decision to present the option of tax-raising powers for the proposed Scottish Parliament as a second question on the ballot paper was seen as a way of defusing a potentially damaging accusation that Scottish devolution would add to the tax burden of people living in Scotland.

(b) They demonstrate that selfish political imperatives often lie behind a decision to hold a referendum. Both sets of referendums also indicate the power of governments to establish the rules of the game, and the totals required for victory. De Tocqueville's argument about the tyranny of the majority is illustrated by the Welsh result in 1997, while both 1997 referendums resulted in an active minority of the electorate imposing its will on the rest of the respective regions.

Useful websites

- The Initiative & Referendum Institute Europe
  www.iri-europe.org
- Democracy International
  www.democracy-international.org
- The Electoral Commission (Focus on: referendums)
  www.electoralcommission.gov.uk/toolkit/theme-listing.cfm/48

Further reading

- McCartney, M. (2002) 'Oh, referenda, where art thou?', *Talking Politics*, vol. 16, no. 1.
- Magee, E. and Outhwaite, D. (2001) 'Referendums and initiatives', *Politics Review*, vol. 10, no. 3.

Glossary

alternative vote plus (AV+)

a combination of the alternative vote (AV) and the additional member system (AMS) recommended by the Independent Commission on Voting Reform as a replacement for the current system for general elections. Weighted heavily in favour of the alternative vote element, its advantages are supposed to include increasing voter choice while maintaining the UK's traditional strong party system.

blog

a website where an individual or group expresses opinions on a particular topic. They first impacted on US elections in 2004, with both sides encouraging their supporters to express their views in this fashion. The more high-profile blogs were sometimes able to influence the campaign agenda by providing the public with partisan interpretations of both main candidates' credibility.

class dealignment

a long-term process where voters no longer maintain a close allegiance to one political party. The causes of dealignment include wider access to higher education, the influence of the media and changes in patterns of work. The chief result of this development has been the creation of a more volatile electorate and the increased importance of issues in shaping voting behaviour.

deviation from proportionality (DV)

the means to compare how far different elections and electoral systems accurately reflect the distribution of votes. To obtain each party's individual DV, you need to subtract the percentage of votes gained from the percentage of seats won. The aggregate score for each party gives you its total DV for that particular election. Non-proportional systems, such as FPTP, have a higher DV than proportional systems.

electoral reform

a campaign to change the system used to elect representatives. In the UK, the electoral reform movement consists of pressure groups such as the Electoral Reform Society, politicians such as the late Robin Cook, and academics.

electronic voting (e-voting)

electronic voting is a process of voting via a computer. This can be done either at home over the internet, or on mobile polling machines. Advocates of e-voting suggest it is a viable means of increasing voter turnout, especially among the young and infirm. Critics argue that this could undermine the principle of the secret ballot and leave the voting system at the mercy of computer hackers.

initiative

unlike conventional referendums, which are government-sponsored, initiatives are called by ordinary citizens. They are commonly used in Switzerland and California.

issue voting

a relatively rare phenomenon in the era of dealignment, associated with rational-choice models of voting. It assumes that voters choose whom to vote for by deciding which party either has the policies closest to their own or is likely to be the most competent in dealing with the most important issues.

majoritarian systems

electoral systems designed to produce an absolute majority of votes for the winning candidate. Examples of this type of system currently in use include alternative vote, supplementary vote and second ballot.

mandate

the right of a party to implement its manifesto promises. A party can claim a mandate to govern when it has won a majority of the popular vote. Mandate theory is less applicable where a proportional electoral system is used, as parties in a coalition would inevitably have to compromise their original policies.

partisan (or party) identification

analysis of UK election results for 1945–70 suggested that most voters had a strong allegiance to a particular party. By identifying with a party, voters were more likely to support its policies and to vote for this party. This resulted in relative electoral stability, with the two main parties receiving over 80% of the vote between them. It also meant that factors such as the performance of a party leader or media influence were relatively insignificant influences on how people voted.

plebiscite

another word for a referendum. Plebiscitary democracy involves extensive use of popular votes on individual issues and is a rarely used alternative to representative democracy.

plurality systems
electoral systems that require a candidate to gain a majority of votes cast in order to get elected. The correct title of the system used for general elections in the UK is 'single member plurality'. It ensures that the winner is quickly known and, as it is not proportional, usually exaggerates the vote share of the leading parties.

proportional systems
electoral systems where the percentage of seats that a party gains is directly proportional to the percentage of votes it wins. PR systems are often used where the intention of the election is to form an assembly broadly representative of different groups in society. Several different types of PR system exist, three of which are used in the UK: closed list, STV and AMS.

protest vote
a form of voting most commonly associated with by-elections and the 'mid-term blues'. Typically, disgruntled voters express their dissatisfaction with the government of the day by electing a candidate from a rival party. When they express their preference at the general election, however, they frequently revert to supporting the party in government.

representative democracy
an attempt to ensure that the popular will is expressed, in a society where citizens lack the time and specialist knowledge to participate directly in decision making themselves. Voters in a constituency elect someone to represent them in a legis-lature. The representatives are accountable to the electorate via regular elections.

tactical voting
a negative form of voting, where voters desert their preferred party to prevent a candidate from their least favourite party winning a seat. During the 1990s, this tactic was targeted against the Conservatives, but the 2005 election saw Labour suffer from Liberal Democrat and Conservative voters shifting allegiance to defeat sitting Labour MPs.

threshold
a device used to prevent a small group of people from having a disproportionate say in a state's decision making. A number of countries insist that a minimum threshold be reached before a referendum is declared legal. This threshold could be a minimum turnout of the electorate or a predetermined percentage of those eligible to vote supporting the proposal. Thresholds can also be used to prevent small parties from gaining seats in a proportional electoral system. In Germany, a party has to obtain at least 5% of the vote, or win one 'constituency' seat, before it is allowed representation in the Reichstag.